HAMPSTEAD HEATH

The Walker's Guide

David McDowall & Deborah Wolton

with sketch maps by Angela Kidner

COVER: *Hampstead Heath*, Charles Sharland, 1914.

First published by David McDowall
31 Cambrian Road, Richmond, Surrey TW10 6JQ

British Library Cataloguing in Publication Data
A catalogue record for this book is available from the British Library

ISBN 0 9527847 1 8

Designed and typeset in Monotype Formata and Octavian by Peter Moore
Printed by Headley Brothers Ltd, Ashford, Kent

Contents

Maps

Illustrations

Figures

Acknowledgements

THE ILLUSTRATIONS

The illustrations listed below have been reproduced with the kind permission of: The Bodleian Library, University of Oxford, p.112 (Kenwood, Hampstead. MssEng. Misc g 68 p.14), p.117 (Johnson Alm. 14 p. 10 Erskine House from the *Polite Repository*, 1795); The British Library, p.123 (K.Top 30.28) and the 25" 1st Edition, London Series, OS Map, c.1866 on p.98-99; The Guildhall Library, Corporation of London, p.137; Camden Local Studies and Archives Centre, pp.17,30,36,51,106,121,139,165; London Metropolitan Archives, pp.54,148; London Transport Museum, cover picture and p.34; The Rt Hon the Earl of Mansfield, p.115; David Sullivan, p.88; V & A Picture Library, p.53; Averil Hassall, copyright untraced, p.62.

THE WORDS

The text could not possibly have been written without substantial help from written sources, primarily those listed in the bibliography on p.168. In addition we are grateful to John Murray (Publishers) Ltd for their kind permission to quote from *Summoned by Bells*, by John Betjeman.

THE PEOPLE

However, it is to the helpfulness of many organisations and individuals that we owe our greatest debt. First, we are grateful to the staff of various organisations: the Barnet Local Studies and Archives Centre, the Camden Local Studies and Archives Centre, the Colson Stone Partnership, English Heritage, English Nature, the London Library, the London Metropolitan Archives and the London

Natural History Society. We should like to record our gratitude to particular individuals: Paul Canneaux (Superintendent of Hampstead Heath), Richard Payne and other Corporation of London staff on Hampstead Heath, and to Kevin Milne of English Heritage at Kenwood, who all answered our queries and made information or research material available. We are particularly grateful to Land Use Consultants whose survey work on the Heath has been an invaluable source.

We are also indebted to others whose work or knowledge we have drawn upon: Noel Hill (the Pergola); Ray Softly and John Maxwell (invertebrates); Anthony Vaughan and Jeremy Wright (the Heath Extension). Others not only shared their knowledge with us but very kindly undertook to read through parts of what we had written, in particular David Bevan (botany); Eric Robinson (geology), and also Paul Canneaux and Mark Lintell who both read the whole text. We should like to record a special debt, however, to two people: the late Kit Ikin, who repeatedly endured our pestering and answered our queries concerning the Heath's history with terrier-like persistence; and, finally, David Sullivan who, with an unrivalled historical grasp, drew much to our attention and also meticulously read the whole text, saving us from errors of fact or judgement. Responsibility for any errors still in the text is ours alone.

We are also very grateful to others who doggedly tested our walks sometimes in the most inclement weather and asked those simple questions that revealed flaws in our directions or in our commentary: Fenella Brown, Gilly and Saskia Gretton, Angela and Patrick Kidner, Elizabeth Laird, John and Mary McDowall, and Michael Ann Mullen. To each of them also many thanks. They, too, saved us from many mistakes and oversights.

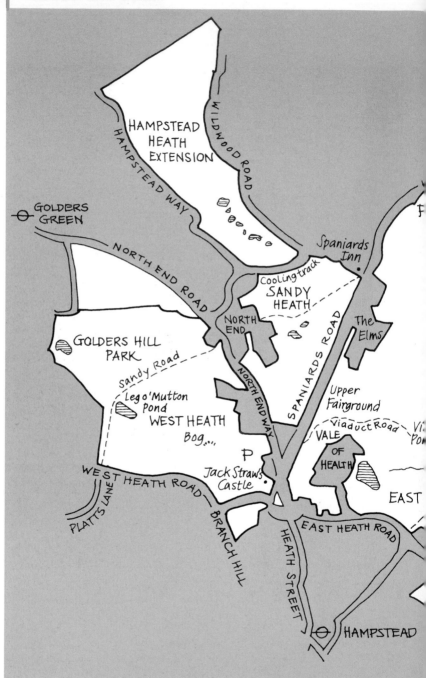

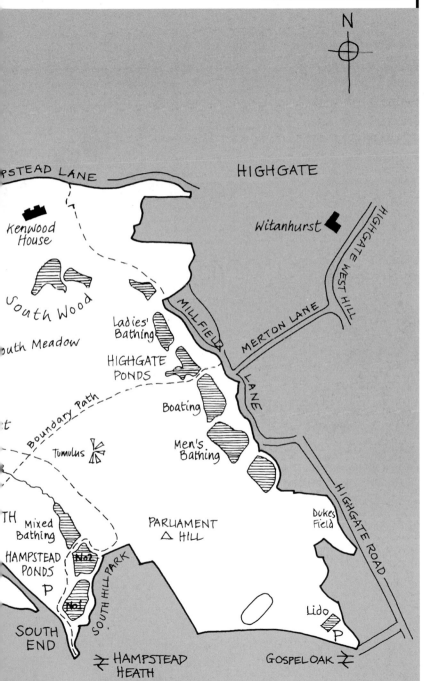

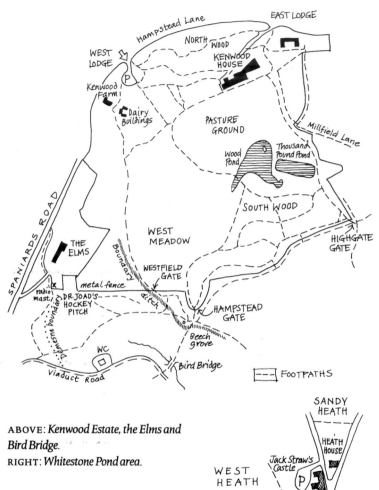

ABOVE: *Kenwood Estate, the Elms and Bird Bridge.*

RIGHT: *Whitestone Pond area.*

Introduction

Hampstead Heath must be the most highly prized open space in London, loved with passion ever since its piecemeal rescue from developers between 1871 and 1925.

This guide is intended to enhance your enjoyment of the Heath. We hope it will help you 'read' the landscape, in particular the inter-connectedness of its geology, ecology and history. Perhaps, like us, you will kick yourself that it took so long to notice many obvious features, but we hope you will also delight in the less obvious ones.

We hope what we have to say will interest, amuse or even surprise you. A few people may be disappointed this guide is not more exhaustive, but our basic intention is to make walking the Heath more rewarding, not to write an encyclopaedia. So we have confined ourselves selfishly to what we find interesting, and consigned the result to a pocket book, not a library shelf.

We have structured our guide into ten walks, in what we think is a logical order for appreciating the evolution of the Heath. We apologise for being so prescriptive, but we hope we may even drag you to a corner of the Heath you have not appreciated before. And if you find our approach too bossy, Walk No. 6 gives you a break, when you are invited to devise your own explorations, based on the hedgerows recorded in the 1860s.

The hardest thing has been to provide clear guidance for each route. With myriad tiny paths and so much undergrowth, this has not been easy but we hope that the sketch maps will suffice where words fail. But, please, never *ever* spoil the pleasure of your walk by spending ages trying to puzzle out shortcomings in our directions, or locate some tiny feature. Both will keep for another day.

David McDowall and Deborah Wolton
June 1998

The geology

shorter walk: 4.5 km / 1.5 hrs
longer walk: 5.25 km / 2.25 hrs

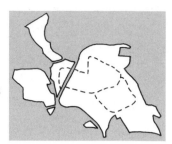

BEFORE YOU WALK

The land between Hampstead and Highgate falls away sharply both
to the south and the north, giving panoramic and spectacular views
in both directions, until trees this century largely obscured the vista
northwards. Known as London's 'Northern Heights', this sandy
tract runs in an arc across the top of the hill, from the upper slopes of
Fitzjohn's Avenue, along the line of the Spaniards Road and
Hampstead Lane, to Highgate.

Appreciating the qualities of this sand, and what lies beneath, is
fundamental to understanding the Heath. This was first publicly
realised by John James Park in his authoritative *Topography and
Natural History of Hampstead* (1814) which he published at the
precocious age of 19:

> 'It has frequently been asked, 'Why is the sand of Hampstead
> confined to the heath? How is it that we do not find sand in
> digging in our fields? Or what is there in the nature of a heath,
> which should make it the *exclusive* depository of such a
> substance?'... The following reply has but lately suggested
> itself to me, but it appears so obvious, and so rational, that
> I am surprised it did not occur on the first blush. It is not,
> I would say, that the sand is confined to the heath but,
> *e converso*, that the heath is confined to the sand, or more
> fully thus: a certain portion of the land has, by some

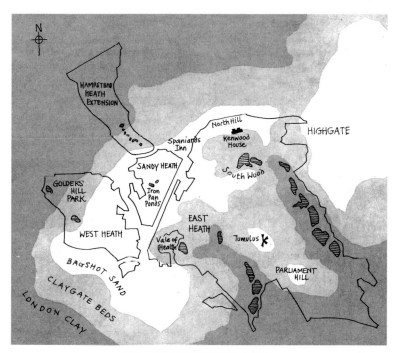

THE GEOLOGY OF THE HEATH

operation of nature, which we suppose to be the action of a
pre-existent ocean, been covered with a bed of sand.'
Park, who died aged only 38, was absolutely right. The
Northern Heights are a sandbank laid down approximately
40 million years ago, the deposit of a vast freshwater river quite as
large as the Ganges, flowing from the western part of Britain. We
know this because the sand contains particles of granite from
Devon. The sand is known geologically as Bagshot Sand, since
Bagshot, in west Surrey, is where this particular riverine deposit
was first identified less than a decade after Park was writing.

Water drains west, north and south from this high ground. The
western side of Hampstead, some way from the Heath, drains into
the Kilburn, known further downstream as the Westbourne, entering

the Thames near Chelsea Bridge. To the north, the Heath's water drains in two main streams via the Leg O'Mutton Pond on West Heath, through Golders Hill, and further east through the Seven Sisters ponds on the Heath Extension. Both streams run into the river Brent, and thence down the Brent valley to the Thames at Brentford. It is, however, the drainage on the southern side which is of greater interest. Two brooks run down the respective Hampstead and Highgate sides of the Heath, both draining into the river Fleet, carrying the principal run-off from the Heath. In between them lies a spur of higher ground including two caps of Bagshot Sand at the Tumulus and on Parliament Hill itself. The rivers Brent, Kilburn and Fleet were rushing torrents two million years ago when they drained much of the outwash from the glacial ice sheet that had reached as far south as Finchley. That is how the two Fleet headwater gullies were cut. These streams are now channelled into culverts, yet given a heavy summer downpour, the Fleet still has the capacity to surprise (see p. 28).

Begin at the Whitestone Pond. The frantic noise of traffic around the Whitestone Pond is a powerful reminder of one of the great attributes of the Heath, its relative quiet. Start walking along the Spaniards Road, along the side wall of Heath House. Just beyond the end of the Heath House garden turn half left down the path onto Sandy Heath.

As you walk down the slope pick up one of the dark smooth pebbles. It is made of flint and came from Wessex, rendered smooth from the river-borne journey it has made. The same flint, but of course not in pebble form, may be found on Salisbury Plain. The Bagshot Sand has several seams of pebbles, the residue of flood episodes while the sand was being laid down. Such pebbles are found all over the Heath, not merely on the high ground where they were originally

laid, since they have been carried downhill by rain and erosion.
(You will also come across amber coloured pebbles, gravel left
by flood rivers in a more recent period of sea floor uplift a mere
13 million years ago.)

**At the bottom of the initial steep section the path divides into
three, left, centre and right. Fork right, passing first a wilding
apple on your left. The second apple tree on your left is
perhaps one of the Heath's true crab apples (see p.32). Follow
the path through the centre of the gorse.**

Watch out for the quality of the sand, which ranges from buff to deep
orange. Where the topsoil is broken the sand underneath is often
golden, ideal builder's sand. Over the centuries this sand was used
for building, for filling in the many potholes in London's streets, and
even for filling sandbags in two world wars. Beyond the gorse the
eerie landscape of craters is the product of hundreds of thousands of
tons of sand being removed. Sandy Heath was originally level with

*Sand digging on Sandy Heath, 1867, with Spaniards Road running along the skyline to
Turner's 'Firs' on the left.*

the Spaniards Road. One of the heaviest periods of extraction took place in the 1860s, during London's most intensive phase of expansion, as *The Illustrated London News* reported in 1871:

> 'The very body of the earth has been cut away to an amazing depth.... Holes are scooped out close to the high road thirty or forty feet deep, and big enough to bury the corpses of a nation for half a century....but ugly enough to deter the boldest survivor from approaching so ghastly a spot.'

Walk across to the larger of the ponds, slightly left of the path.

Most ponds are intentionally man-made (discussed later). These ponds are the accidental result of sand extraction. Being on the very top of the Heath they are neither stream nor spring fed, nor do they drain anywhere. Yet sand could hardly be more porous. The secret to these strange ponds lies in one of the qualities of the Bagshot Sand on the Heath. It has a very heavy iron content. In this particular case iron oxide has assisted in the coalescence of the sand into a hard crust of sandstone, known as an iron pan, lying about a metre beneath the surface.

Turn your back on the larger pond and make your way to the Spaniards Road by the shortest route (make for the sound of the traffic). Cross the Spaniards Road, turn right and find the left turning with a traffic barrier near the bus stop. A tarmac path will lead you down towards the radio mast (see map on p.12). About 20 paces down the tarmac path follow a small footpath leading off to the right to a field known as Dr Joad's Hockey Pitch, after Professor Joad of the BBC Brains Trust. Continue down the slope of Dr Joad's Hockey Pitch. A path runs parallel to your progress on your left, and after about 80 metres it is backed by a metal fence.

This is still Bagshot Sand. You can find the sandy evidence on the roots of the fallen tree at the bottom right hand corner of the Pitch. This, like several other trees on Bagshot Sand, blew down in the great storm of 1987. The sand, unlike clay lower down, was unable to hold the roots. The holes left, which testify to the geology of the terrain, are known as 'Robinson's Pits' after Eric Robinson, the Heath's leading geological exponent. Note the springy 'feel' underfoot of the Bagshot Sand. Late on in the walk as you move downhill onto London Clay the ground will feel heavier, and will lose its 'spring'.

Follow the metal fence on your left for about 180 metres to Westfield Gate. Turn left into West Meadow, following the main gravel path towards Kenwood House.

West Meadow lies at the beginning of an intermediate layer of sand and clay between the Bagshot Sand above, and London Clay the principal geological characteristic of the lower Thames Valley. It is a good place to note the finer narrow bladed grasses of sandy soil beginning to give way to coarser bladed grasses, indicating the changing geology. This intermediate layer, known as the Claygate Beds (first so identified at Claygate in Surrey in 1912) is principally sandy at the top and progressively more clayish below. This is because a greater proportion of sand settled in the shallower part of the sea that once covered the area about 50 million years ago, about 10 million years before the deposit of Bagshot Sand. The Claygate Beds on Hampstead Heath are possibly thicker than elsewhere.

Like the Bagshot Sand, the Claygate Beds are porous at the top of the stratum, but less so further down towards the London Clay. The consequence is that water draining through the Claygate Beds is apt to hit an impermeable layer of clay and to move horizontally, 'springing' out of the sloping ground. This is the explanation for all those muddy patches on hilly parts of the Heath. Most springs are close to the transition to London Clay, but not all.

Look to your right at the two shallow gullies on West Meadow. In both cases water has hit thin layers of pipe clay (so named for its fine quality suitable for tobacco-smoking pipes) in the upper level of the Claygate Beds. (You may safely impress your friends by talking airily of this feature as a 'perched water table'.) These gullies are perennially wet, essential to some of the flora to be found there. Known to the cognoscenti as an 'acidic flush', the Southern (fenced) gully is the only place in London where you may find a community of sphagnum moss, horsetail and water pepper. Because of its antiseptic qualities, sphagnum was used for wound dressings during the First World War.

After passing the Dairy on your left, fork right to the gate into the Pasture Ground, cross the main path and walk across the greensward (passing the Henry Moore) towards the Stone Bridge on the right of Wood Pond.

As you make your way down the slope, glance back to your left at Kenwood House standing on its terrace. Although the terrace has been sculpted, its foot marks the actual transition from Bagshot Sand to Claygate Beds. In fact, on the north side of the House the Bagshot Sand rises to North Hill, between the House and Hampstead Lane (where Walk No. 2 will take you). Indeed, the quarry (currently not accessible to the public) on the West Drive provides the best example of the layers of Bagshot Sand interrupted by flood strata of pebbles.

Stop on the Stone Bridge.

Glance to your left at Wood Pond, fed by the uppermost reaches of this tributary of the river Fleet. This is a man-made excavation, probably the seventeenth century enlargement of four medieval fish ponds (identified when Wood Pond was cleaned). It was probably originally made by 'puddling'. Puddling is the labour-intensive but effective precursor to butyl rubber. Essentially one either digs down to, or lays, clay to form the base of a pond. Since this is high on the Claygate Beds it is likely that clay had to be brought up from the site of the Highgate Ponds. The clay then had to be 'trodden in', an arduous task rather like kneading bread, to form a compressed and relatively impervious membrane. Sheep or other livestock were often driven onto such clay layers to assist the process.

Now look on the right hand side of the bridge and note the orange coloration (barely visible after long dry periods) in the water under the bank on the right. This coloration marks where water off the Bagshot Sand runs into the stream. It has a heavy iron content, hence its rust colour. The quality of water of the Bagshot Sand varies enormously. In some places Hampstead's springs produce pure soft and lime-free water, for example at Shepherd's Fields (the defunct fountain marking the spring at the junction of Fitzjohn's Avenue and Lyndhurst Road). Elsewhere it has an iron salt content, in the form of iron carbonate, iron oxide and iron sulphate. Known as 'chalybeate', these waters according to Park, were 'of the same nature and equal in virtue with Tunbridge Wells' and used as a purgative.

In 1698 Hampstead's lady of the manor granted to trustees acting for the parish poor six acres of land of Heath containing springs to erect spa buildings. It was not long before an even larger area, from New End down more or less to Willow Road, had been built upon. The original intention had been to sell flasks of water in

London (hence possibly the name Flask Walk) but it was not long before Londoners were flocking to Hampstead Wells to take the waters, now commemorated in the name Well Walk, though the main spring was slightly higher up the hill. Some people can be prudish about their bowels, but not a certain Doctor Soame who in 1734 reported that he 'had experienced relief in a most obstinate and painful case of stone by use of its waters, and that he constantly *shaved* in them.' Had this water proved unsatisfactory for shaving Soame would, no doubt, have resorted to the Kilburn's waters which were said, according to Park, 'to be good against all scorbutic humours, blotches, redness and pimples in the face ...' The craze for Hampstead spa water persisted for much of the eighteenth century.

Go through South Wood to Highgate Gate: from the Stone Bridge bear left at the first three choices, and turn right at the fourth, and then proceed straight to Highgate Gate. Continue straight out along the tarmac path for 50m and then veer left down the earth path into the Highgate Brook gully (with the Ladies Bathing and Bird Sanctuary Ponds on your left) to the gap in the trees at the bottom.

By the time you have reached the bottom of the gully you will have descended from Claygate Beds to London Clay. The ground will feel much heavier underfoot here, compared with the springier sandy soil above. London Clay was laid down approximately 60 million years ago, as a fine silty mud deposit of a warm sea. It is about 120 metres in thickness (below that is about 200 metres of Chalk, and below that lies Devonian rock). On the surface the clay is an ochre colour, the result of oxidation. But below the surface, it is greyish blue. Fossils in the clay suggest a climate similar to, say, Florida today, with the landscape characterised by palm trees and swamps. It is the ability of clay particles to hold water between them that makes the lower parts of the Heath so muddy. For most of the year the gap in the trees at the bottom of the gully is a good example of how muddy it can get.

Walk half right through the gap to an old tree trunk lying among some young poplars on the hillside about 100m away.

Beside this tree trunk is particularly green grass and a good example of one of Hampstead Heath's many springs where the Claygate Beds meet London Clay. Except in high summer, it can be very muddy.

You have a choice. This walk now takes you back to the Whitestone Pond. But if you wish to walk further and explore the story of the Fleet (and the Highgate and Hampstead Ponds), turn to p.26. Otherwise, walk up to the grassy knoll with the small clump of trees about 100 metres away.

The trees of this clump, a beech, a lime and a Tree of Heaven (*Ailanthus*), were clearly planted to enhance the view, part of the London County Council's controversial attempt to turn rustic meadow into public park at the turn of the century. There is a good view from here across to Canary Wharf.

Walk uphill towards the Tumulus (see p.143 if you are intrigued by this enigmatic feature), just short of which is a tarmac path which you should join, bearing right. After nearly 300m you will reach the junction of many paths and a No Cycling notice.

Just before reaching the junction you may note on your right one of a few copper beeches on the Heath. They are not everyone's favourite. Alan Mitchell, author of Collins' *Field Guide to the Trees of Britain*, abhorred 'the heavy, dark, blackish-purple colour which disfigures so much of our landscape. Grossly overplanted in villages, rectory gardens, churchyards, parks and all commemorative plantings. Only 'River's Purple' a superior dark red form can, occasionally, be excused.' So now you know.

Turn left at the junction and walk down the Boundary Path, the avenue running past the side of the Football Pitch. Walk down the Boundary Path for a good 200m to the bottom of the gully. Once over the stream, turn half right up the track.

By this stage you will have become so geologically sensitive (or have we failed?) that you will notice immediately that as you climb up the steep section of track you have left the London Clay of the stream bed level behind and are back on Claygate Beds. The Hampstead Brook, this stream, is the natural primary feeder for the Hampstead Ponds.

Continue on this track climbing the valley-side, passing the Parent and Children's enclosure on your left, and on to the south east corner of the Vale of Health Pond. Here turn right, along the path across the embankment earth barrage.

The Vale of Health was an unhealthy swamp until 1777 when the Hampstead Water Company drained it in order to make a new reservoir (in addition to the Hampstead Ponds). Once drained it became a popular location and was developed in the nineteenth century.

Turn left at the barrier across the track, and go between the massive apartment block of Spencer House (how did they get away with it?) on your left and the caravan site on your right. Turn left at the end of Byron Villas, and take your first turn to

the right just beyond another apartment block, Atheneum Hall, on your left. Walk past the Villas on the Heath, towards what looks like a dead-end, but you will find you can then turn right along the footpath down the side of the villas. When you emerge on the Heath again, go half left across the carriageway up the hillside, through the gorse to the group of pines at the top.

If you look carefully as you ascend back to the Whitestone Pond, you will see ripples on the hillside. Bagshot Sand is notoriously unstable, and these are earthslips. You may wonder what large apartment mansions are doing overlooking the Vale of Health. Even the heavy traffic around the Whitestone Pond can cause instability.

One final point. The hard and soft water locally available made Hampstead an ideal location for the washing and starching of linen. From the Tudor period through to the nineteenth century, Londoners sent their dirty laundry to the washerwomen of Hampstead, many of whom dried their clean linen on the gorse bushes that then dominated the landscape.

Return to the Whitestone Pond.

ADDITIONAL WALK

The story of the Fleet

(this adds 1 km / 45 mins to your walk.)

Join the path running down the west side of the Highgate Ponds. Pause between the Model Boating Pond and the Men's Bathing Pond.

We do not know precisely how old the Highgate Ponds are, but in their present form they were probably dug between 1690 and 1710, and certainly by 1744. They were reservoirs for the supply of potable water to London. Before then there may well have been fish ponds, duly dug and probably puddled. The puddling would have been much easier down here than in the case of Wood Pond, since the ground is already London Clay. The ponds were still supplying water to London in the early years of the nineteenth century. Pipes made of hollowed elm were used to convey water in the seventeenth and eighteenth centuries, and remains of these were found below the Highgate Ponds during excavations in the mid-nineteenth century (and another found even above the Viaduct Pond in the 1970s).

In all probability there was also once a watermill. How else would Millfield Lane have been so called? The valley and the high ground south of the Tumulus was already called Millfield when this parcel of land was established as a farm separate from the rest of the Kenwood estate to the north in 1525. It is just possible that the name refers to a windmill but, apart from the very dubious theory concerning the Tumulus (see p. 143), no nearby windmill site has been definitively identified. Besides, a watermill is more likely given the regular energy source provided by the stream.

We know that the river Fleet (or more anciently the Holebourne, or 'stream in the hollow' – hence Holborn) had many watermills in the middle ages. In about 1180 a monk, William FitzStephen, referred to streams to the north of London 'on which stand many a mill whose clack is delightful to the ear.' In 1307 the earl of Lincoln complained that:

> 'whereas in times past the course of water, running at London under Oldebourne bridge and Fleete bridge into the Thames, had been of such breadth and depth, that ten or twelve ships navies at once, with merchandise, were wont to come to the foresaid bridge of the Fleete, and some of them to Oldbourne bridge; now the same course ... was sore decayed ... also ... by diversion of the water the name of river ceased, and since then called a brook, namely turnmill or Tremill brook, for that divers mills were erected upon it.'

Walk down to the lowest (No.1) Pond.

Notice the willow wands sprouting from the stakes around the edges of the pond. The large bank at the bottom end of the pond is partly spoil from an unsuccessful attempt to dig an artesian well on the site of William Ellis School in 1853. The French engineers contracted for the job bored to a depth of 1302 feet but failed to strike a water reservoir beneath.

After passing the pond turn right, climb the hill and follow the tarmac path that runs across on the south side and just below the summit of Parliament Hill. Pause on the spur where there is a good view of the Lido and Athletics Track.

The two tributaries of the Fleet originally met further south, by Hawley Road in Camden Town. More water, of course, ran straight off Parliament Hill and in the mid-nineteenth century it was still possible to buy watercress from the cress beds where the North London Line now runs.

The headwaters of the Fleet now seem modest trickles. But an anchor has been found in the river bed in lower Kentish Town, suggesting it may once have been navigable up to the confluence of the two feeder streams. In the early nineteenth century the Highgate Brook was 13 foot wide where it crossed the Highgate Road, just beside Dukes Field. When the Fleet flooded in 1826, it was 65 foot wide where the two tributaries met. After it was channelled underground, the Fleet became a source of sickness. In the 1950s the Hampstead General Hospital traced the trail of its chronic bronchitis cases to the course of Hampstead Brook, down the axis of Malden Road. Since then the Hampstead Brook has been channelled underground across the bottom of Parliament Hill Fields to join the Highgate Brook, underground from the ponds, in front of the Lido.

The Fleet is still a force to be reckoned with. A freak summer storm in August 1975 rapidly overflowed the drains intended to take the water and flooded the houses of Oak Village at Gospel Oak, the Vale of Health at the head of Hampstead Brook, and along South End Road. Similar floods occurred in West End Lane, along the course of the Kilbourne. Mind you, no less than 6.72 inches of rain fell in three hours.

Continue along the path swinging to the right when you reach the houses of Tanza Road/Parliament Hill. Pass the top end of the road named Parliament Hill. Follow the path along the rear wall of the back gardens of South Hill Park, and turn left along a main tarmac path just after the garden wall itself turns left. Follow this path down to the causeway between the Hampstead Mixed Bathing and No. 2 Ponds.

A potable water supply became an increasing problem as London grew. The City Corporation had been responsible for adequate

supplies since the thirteenth century, if not earlier. In 1544
Henry VIII's parliament provided for the tapping of the headwaters
of the Fleet as a result of the Mayor of London's feasibility study.
He had:

> 'not onely by diligent searche and exploracion, founde out
> dyvers great and plentyfull sprynges at Hampstede-heath,
> Marybone, Hackney, Muswell-hylle, and divers places
> within five miles of the saide citie, very meete, propise, and
> convenient to be brought and conveyed to the same; but also
> hath laboured, studied, and devised the conveyance thereof,
> by cundytes, vautes, and pipes, to the said citie, and
> otherwise ... .'

The Mayor of London was duly empowered to lay pipes, dig pits
and erect conduits to exploit the springs on the Heath, although a
plan for 'drawing diverse springes about Hampsted heath into one
head and course' was only made in 1589. The scheme was, however,
a failure. Apparently the 'banks gave way so much and so much soil
was cast thereby into the stream that it became worse cloyed and
choken than before.' That 'head' was in all probability the reservoir
dug on the lower Heath below the present Hampstead ponds on the
ground alongside South End Road, opposite the foot of Keat's Grove.
This, the oldest pond, was abandoned after it had become putrid,
and was filled with spoil in 1892.

The Corporation of London had to take care where it tapped
Hampstead's water for the 1544 Act protected Hampstead's
interests:

> 'the saide maior and comminaltie, or their successours shall
> not, at any tyme hereafter, medle with the springes at the foote
> of the hyll of the sayde heath called Hamsted-heth nowe
> closed in with bricke, for the ease, commoditie and necessary
> use of the inhabitants of the towne of Hamstede.'

The pumphouse on South End Road, c.1905.

In 1682 a Hampstead Water Company leased the springs and then dug new ponds and reservoirs. These were probably more or less as we now see them. The Highgate and Hampstead Ponds supplied water to Kentish Town and Camden Town for 150 years. By the 1830s the yield from the ponds was insufficient for the rapidly increasing demand, and a 400 foot well was sunk at the foot of East Heath Road, beside Hampstead No. 1 Pond. A steam pump brought the water to the surface, housed in an octagonal tower which was demolished in 1907.

At the far end of the causeway (the west side) follow the path up the steep bank and around to the right along the side of the pond enclosure, following the path back to the Boundary Path. Follow the rest of the walk back to the Whitestone Pond as described on p.23.

The trees and woodlands

WALK 2

4.5 km / 2 hrs

This walk explores the Heath's landscape through its ancient and more recent secondary woodland, its boundary and hedgerow trees, and the specimen and exotic species planted as part of the eighteenth and nineteenth century landscapes.

Start at the car park behind Jack Straw's Castle. Take the pathway leading onto West Heath which is a continuation of the Car Park entrance road. Continue straight on downhill for about 200m to the spring and ponds and surrounding boggy area.

As the ice retreated at the end of the last ice age about 12,000 years ago, the climate of Britain became progressively warmer, and trees gradually recolonized the country from the south. Because it is permanently waterlogged, West Heath bog has conserved vital evidence of what the prehistoric landscape was like. Surviving pollen, seed and insect remains extracted from a depth of two metres below the surface of this bog indicate the kind of forest or 'wildwood' (known as 'Atlantic forest') covering the country by about 5000 BC. They confirm that, like much of lowland England, the forest was dominated by both small and large leafed limes, oak, hazel and alder.

Follow the stream about 300m downhill towards the Leg O'Mutton Pond.

We know of at least one nearby human settlement in the 'Mesolithic' (post-glacial) period. As the human population grew and turned from hunting and gathering to cultivation at the beginning of the Neolithic period, around 3500 BC, the wildwood was increasingly and permanently cleared. Pollen samples of this period from West Heath reveal a sharp decline in elm trees, possibly caused by elm disease since remains of the fungus-carrying beetle were found in the sample. The clearing of the wildwood was followed by progressive increase in cereals, grasses and heathland plants, and the appearance of dung beetles, indicative of livestock rearing. Thus we can dimly picture the scene by, say, 2000 BC, of major forest clearance, the domestication of livestock, rudimentary cereal production, and because of the acid sandy soils, the formation of heathland. By 500 BC half of England had probably ceased to be woodland, an astonishing feat given how difficult it is to clear mature forest. By the time of the Norman Conquest 1500 years later virtually none of this original 'wildwood' was left. However, it had not all been grubbed out; some of it had been turned into managed woodland.

It is likely that a large part of the West Heath remained heathland with a central boggy area from prehistoric times up to the 1880s. That horse-racing was a popular sport on West Heath in the early eighteenth century indicates how treeless it must have been at that time.

On your right, on the north side of the pond you should find an old apple tree.

This may be a true and now relatively rare wild crab, one of a few surviving descendants of the group of crab apples which were virtually the only tree cover when much of the West Heath was still largely open heathland in the late nineteenth century. Or it may be a 'wilding', of which there are several on the heath, sprung from the pip of a domestic apple.

Just beyond the apple turn sharply to your right and follow the gully back up the slope towards the west side of the Hill Garden.

The existing secondary woodland has grown up since grazing, digging of sand and cutting of turfs ceased in the late nineteenth century. This 'succession' from heathland to mixed woodland has all occurred in the past century. Birch, the most common tree on West Heath is a pioneer on acid soil. Like other pioneers it produces large numbers of wind-borne seeds, but it cannot tolerate shade and does not survive as an understorey tree. Holly, the other commmon tree here, is both a pioneer and a thriving survivor, since it does not mind shade, even under a canopy of mature oak and beech.

The vegetation here is evolving towards climax woodland. The colonisers are still here, but the birch trees are now close to the end of their life span of eighty to a hundred years. In places one can see dead birch beneath the now higher canopy. But the pattern of lime domination of the Atlantic forest will not be repeated. In other parts of the country there are still some ancient lime woods but they do not spread back into areas where they once were, probably because of climatic change, or their place has been taken by hornbeams.

When you reach the wall of the Hill Garden, turn left and follow the boundary which will lead you to Inverforth Close.

As you walk along the path known as Inverforth Close the site of the two Gibbet Elms (see p.131) is on your left, where the corpse of a highwayman, Francis Jackson, hung for many years after his capture. Jackson, *alias* Dixie, was one of a gang of five who had attacked the Windsor coach near Heathrow on Hounslow Heath in May 1674. They knew that if they could slip into the city they could lose any pursuers. But the hue

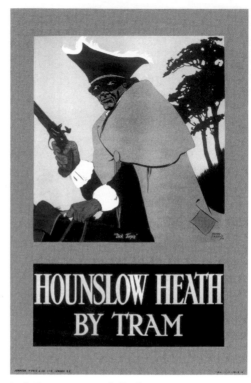

London Transport poster, 1914, by Tony Sarg.

Getting into London is easier now

and cry had been truly raised, and each time they approached London they were turned back by vigilantes, first at Acton and after a detour to Harrow-on-the-Hill, again at Paddington. They tried again *via* Hendon. Just after passing North End they were ambushed where you are now standing. Jackson and his comrades were almost certainly ex-soldiers for, although their powder and shot was spent, they managed to hold off their attackers, said to have numbered 200 local men, for nearly an hour. Before they surrendered Jackson had slain a man. It was for this reason that his corpse subsequently hung here after he had been hanged. He was still on the scene in 1691 when an unsavoury but no doubt accurate ditty was published:

As often upon Hampstead Heath,
Have seen a felon long since put to death,
Hang crackling in the sun his parchment skin
Which to his ear had shrivell'd up his chin.

The last of the Gibbet Elms blew down in 1907. Until disease virtually wiped them out in the 1970s, elms were common on the Heath. Their great billowing forms had towered over other trees for centuries. In several places in old hedgerows you can find the stumps of great elms, evidence of how dominant these trees must have been with their heavy masses of dark foliage:

'.... rich elms careering down the hill,
Full billows rolling into Holloway.'

(John Betjeman)

The most recent epidemic of elm disease has been so virulent that an estimated 20 million elms have died since 1960, and the English elm, as a mature tree, has become a memory.

As you emerge onto North End Way turn right and walk about 25 paces and then cross the road. This will take you into an avenue of lime trees. Continue down the avenue for a short distance then, as it swings to the left, bear slightly right and continue through the woodland for about 200m until you come to the 'iron pan' ponds (see p.18).

Sandy Heath has a similar history to that of West Heath. Once covered in Atlantic forest, it was progressively cleared from Neolithic times. Heathland developed and was maintained over the centuries by grazing, cutting and the digging of sand and turf. Although a number of trees were planted in the eighteenth century,

Two Tree Hill, 1866. These trees are still here, to the east of the largest 'iron pan' pond, with the Firs in the distance. The remains of a metal collar on one of the trees indicates that they were probably braced together to stabilize them.

and some old pollards survive from the time of the common, most of Sandy Heath is secondary woodland established since the Heath became public property in 1871, with pioneer birch giving way to oak and beech.

Sandy Heath has a very particular character, with dips and hollows of sand workings. In the south east section where the most recent sand digging took place, there is an eerie atmosphere created with almost bare earth under a closed canopy of oak. Some oaks were too well established to be dug up easily and sand was dug away from around them, leaving them perched on hillocks, sometimes with their roots uncomfortably exposed.

Join Sandy Road and turn right, walking towards the Spaniards.

This stretch of Sandy Road was made by a Mr Turner, a retired Fleet Street tobacconist, who lived at 'The Firs' (now called 'The Chantry'), the large house on the left as you approach the Spaniards. Until the beginning of the twentieth century Sandy Road was a public route for vehicles linking the Spaniards through North End to Child's Hill.

When you can see the end of Sandy Road (about 100m away), you will see on your left what seems to be the last remaining 'fir' of a group planted in about 1745 by Turner. The trees were not true firs but Scots pine raised, it is said, from seed gathered from La Pineta, the forest of Ravenna extolled by Dante, Boccaccio and Byron. Turner acted with unwitting prescience. La Pineta, which existed at the time of the Ostrogoths in the fifth century AD and probably much earlier, was largely destroyed by a severe winter in 1880/81, and by forest fire. Only a remnant, threatened by industrial development, survives. Turner's 'Firs' remained a well known landmark throughout the nineteenth century, frequently drawn and painted. It shows how much the tree cover has changed that people came here to admire the view across to Harrow-on-the-Hill. Just beyond Turner's 'Firs' there are two spectacular old coppiced beeches, survivors from the time this was common land.

Turner had responded to a growing fashion for pines as a picturesque feature,

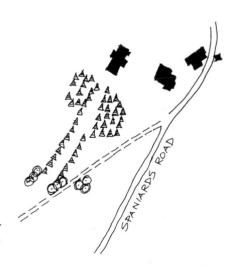

TURNER'S 'FIRS' C. 1850

inspired no doubt by rediscovery of the landscape and ruins of classical Italy, Greece and even Lebanon (hence the craze elsewhere for cedars of Lebanon). Pines were planted on the Tumulus in the eighteenth century, and two surviving clumps were planted in the 1780s on promontories in the north east corner of West Heath by the owner of Golders Hill. He was instructed by the manor court to remove them, but seems to have ignored this.

In April and May look out for native bluebells with their dark blue drooping flowers and slim leaves. The native bluebell is now quite rare on the Heath. What is more commonly seen is the vigorous and paler blue hybrid, a cross between the native and Spanish bluebell.

Leave Sandy Heath at the Spaniards and turning left walk along Hampstead Lane towards Kenwood House.

As you walk through the narrow gap at the Spaniards you are passing through the 'Park Gate' of what was once the bishop of London's deer park or Hornsey Park (see p.76). The southern boundary of the deer park coincided with the old parish boundary. Although the main purpose of a deer park was the supply of venison, it would often provide other products as well, most commonly wood.

Managed woodlands were a vital resource for medieval society, providing fuel, underwood and timber. We know that thousands of fuel faggots were extracted annually from this park, and the demand, bearing in mind London's proximity, must have been considerable. Timber would have been extracted for any heavy purpose: the construction of housing, the making of carts, ploughs and so forth. 'Underwood' was also vital, cut mainly from coppiced trees, usually hazel, hornbeam, field maple or alder that were regularly harvested to provide the basic material for 'wattle',

COPPICE STOOL   THE SPRING   A LAPSED COPPICE

for fencing or the infilling of timber-frame houses, and for almost every conceivable wooden implement.

The woodland areas would have been managed as coppice, divided into 'falls' or plots, to be cut in rotation. The 'spring' (the shoots) was cut at varying intervals, depending on the purpose for which it was required.

Enter Kenwood Estate through the second gate of the West Lodge entrance. Follow the footpath immediately off to your left which winds through North Wood to the East Lodge. (See p.12 for map of Kenwood Estate.)

The pines here were probably planted at the suggestion of Humphry Repton (see p. 110) towards the end of the eighteenth century. He was keen on conifers. This small piece of woodland is two quite different woods divided by the path. The section between the path and Hampstead Lane is naturally regenerated secondary woodland bounded by a row of Turkey oaks planted when the road was moved away from the front of Kenwood House to its present route in the 1790s (see p.76). Turkey oaks then were a relatively new arrival in Britain having been introduced in 1735. They were widely planted probably because of their very rapid growth and longevity. They are distinguishable by the long twisted whiskers surrounding their buds and by their whiskery acorn cups.

TURKEY OAK

The woodland on the south side of the path goes back to the time it was part of the medieval deer park. The trees themselves are not more than 300 years at the most, but this patch has been woodland since the middle ages. Writing in about 1180 the London-born monk, William FitzStephen, noted:

> 'close by on the north side of London lies an immense forest in which are densely wooded thickets, the coverts of game, red and fallow deer, boars and wild bulls.'

By the time of FitzStephen, however, this 'immense forest', fancifully called the Ancient Forest of Middlesex, was no longer a great tract of virgin forest as he romatically implies. But extensive woods there certainly were, valuable property held by a variety of landlords or tenants, yielding timber and underwood, or managed as wood pasture or game reserves. A number of woods, including Bishop's Wood within the deer park were leased and many of them seem to have survived up to the eighteenth century, providing the materials for construction, fencing, tools and firewood. Turner's Wood, close to the Heath Extension (see p.153) was probably one of them. Several references have been found to supplies of timber from Hornsey woods; one dated 1406 lists 32 spars for the belfry of St Paul's Cathedral, and 1000 faggots of firewood.

From the East Lodge continue down the path marked 'To Restaurant' through the holly, laurel and rhododendron, which leads to the east side of the kitchen wing.

As you walk down the hill you cross the southern boundary of the Bishop's deer park, which is also the boundary between the parishes of Hornsey and St Pancras (see p.76).

Continue walking down the hill and turn right onto the terrace of Kenwood House.

Straight ahead stands a very fine London plane tree planted in about 1770 by William Murray, first Earl of Mansfield. This tree is a hybrid between the Oriental and American planes, and is a perfect example of hybrid vigour. Contrary to its name, it probably originated in southern Europe in about 1650, but it could have been 'designed' for London, so well suited is it to city life, unlike either of its parents. It withstands drought, compacted soil, polluted air, it is resistant to diseases and rarely blows down. And it is grand in scale. One of the first to be planted in England in about 1680, still stands in the garden of the Bishop's Palace, Ely, full of vigour.

Walk along the terrace then down the steps on your left onto the lawn and down towards the Wood Pond.

In both the eighteenth and nineteenth centuries many landed proprietors became avid collectors of exotic species of trees and shrubs. The Mansfields were among them. Slightly to the left as one looks down the lawn stands a Caucasian elm, or Zelkova, a large multi-stemmed tree with smooth grey bark. Planted in the 1760s, this must have been one of the very first specimens brought into the country. One can imagine William Murray proudly showing the young tree to his guests.

Slightly to the right, dead centre in front of the lake, stands a nineteenth century addition, the Swamp or Bald cypress, introduced from the swamplands of the southern United States. It is unusual in that it is a deciduous conifer, and one of the last trees to come into leaf, thereby no doubt acquiring its epithet, 'Bald'. The Swamp cypress stands as a warning that in maturity erstwhile saplings no longer grace a view as once they did.

Turning left, walk around the north side of Wood Pond and Thousand Pound Pond and into South Wood. Once in the wood take a path to your right and wander through the wood, heading for Hampstead Gate.

Along with North Wood, South Wood has been designated a Site of Special Scientific Interest (SSSI), partly because both are long established high forest woodlands, but also because their dead wood, both standing and lying, provides a habitat for invertebrates. Most terrestrial invertebrate species depend on decaying wood in some form at some stage in their life cycle. For many of these dead wood inhabiting — saproxylic — creatures, old trees such as these with their stag-headed branches, rot holes and cavities are a last refuge in an over-tidy world. Arguably more damage was done to woodland habitats in the clearing-up process than was done by the great storm itself in October 1987.

South Wood is certainly ancient, that is, it existed in 1600. It may also be 'semi-natural', in other words a remnant of the natural wood which evolved in prehistoric times before coming under human management. Its status as ancient woodland is supported by a range of indicator species, among them the wild service tree (see below).

The sessile (or durmast) oak which grows on light and acid soils is common in the north and west of the country but rarer in the south east. It is very similar to the other native oak, the common or

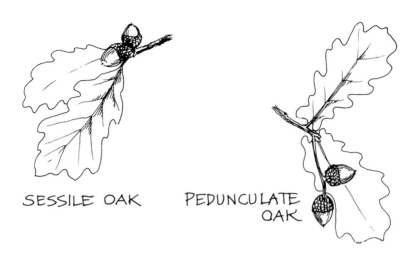

SESSILE OAK PEDUNCULATE OAK

pedunculate oak, which grows on clays and other heavier soils of the lowlands. But the sessile has never been planted in the way that the common oak has been and is largely confined to the areas it must have occupied in the wildwood. Their names suggest the way to tell them apart, for 'sessile' means 'without stalk'. The acorn of the sessile oak has only a very short stalk while the acorn of the common oak has a long stalk (or peduncle). However, there is some contrariness about them in that the leaf of the common oak has a *short* stalk while the sessile leaf has a *long* stalk. To make matters more difficult, the two frequently hybridise.

The common oak was favoured because it usually produces more acorns and because its naturally angled branches were more useful to medieval builders. The tree is characteristically round-headed with a multitude of zig-zag twigs with heavier branches formed like giant elbows, full of curves and angles and a rich variety of shapes. These were ideally suited for the crucks of houses, the hulls of ships and a great number of structural functions for which it was superceded by iron and steel in the nineteenth century. By contrast, the sessile oak is usually a straight trunked and lofty tree when grown in good conditions. The huge straight beams in Westminster Hall are probably sessile oak. (Incidentally, after bomb damage in 1941 replacement timbers came from the same estate as the original fourteenth century beams).

The beech here may also be growing naturally. Hampstead is certainly within the beech's natural region, but on the other hand it was a highly fashionable tree to plant in the eighteenth and nineteenth centuries.

We know that in the sixteenth century the Kenwood estate was divided into two. The part southwards from the hedgerow just south of the Tumulus, now known as Parliament Hill Fields, was farmland in the early sixteenth century. The northern part consisted of two woods, Cane Wood and Gyll Holt (or Gillishawte). There seems to have been no marked division between these two woods, but it is likely that Gyll Holt lay in the upper part of valley containing the present Highgate Ponds. In the late Saxon and medieval periods the name was used to indicate a wooded valley, usually with a stream. It would probably have contained willows and alders, contrasting with the oak trees which probably gave Cane Wood its name. *Keyne* is the Norman French word for oak, an indicator that the name is early medieval. The two woods extended from the hedgerow just south of the Tumulus northwards to the boundary with Bishop's Park, and in the west from the boundary with Hampstead Manor across to Millfield Lane to the east (see map on p.64).

Here we get a real idea of the coppicing regime, for a map has survived from the period which shows the whole wood as divided into ten 18-acre plots 'of diverse groathes with the value of evearie fall at Tenne yeares groath', the reckonable values being duly recorded for each plot. In other words, the woodland was thinnned or felled on a ten-year rotation, plot by plot. If Kenwood was like other woodlands, it was probably coppiced in the middle ages on a more frequent rotation of about seven years. Timber would also have been removed. But cropping did not always go according to plan, and another entry on the map reads, 'Note there was 500 principals [timber trees] felled at the last fall which by the Status ought to have been preserved ...'

Wander through the woodland and head for Hampstead Gate.

As you approach the gate look at the edge of the wood on your left, where you will see stretches of the earth bank that was the boundary of the old wood. Sometime after 1600 a large part of the two woods had been felled and converted into open fields. This bank probably dates from this time, as the boundary of the much reduced woodland. By the mid-seventeenth century Kenwood was a gentleman's residence and South Wood, although it continued to be a productive wood, was from now on cherished for the beauty of its trees and as an adornment to the estate.

Walk out of South Wood through Hampstead Gate. Walk straight across the path towards the old boundary oak.

Hedgerow and boundary oaks are the oldest trees on the Heath, but it is difficult to be sure of the age of a growing tree, without a record of its planting. The height and spread of a tree reaches a maximum size but then begins to decrease. But the bole or trunk continues to increase every year of its life as it lays down an annual ring of wood. These particular oaks, just outside Hampstead Gate, appear to have been pollarded at some stage (see p.93), but it is impossible to be sure of their age without felling them. Unlike continental Europe, Britain is a country of old trees, where since the seventeenth century, if not earlier, they have been valued and admired. In many places in

Britain 400 year-old oaks are not uncommon. One oak in Suffolk has been estimated to be 1,000 years old.

Walk down the hill passing the large oak on your right, towards the Bird Bridge. On your left you will pass a grove of beeches planted in the mid-nineteenth century by the Hampstead lord of the manor.

If you walk through this wood when the beech are in full leaf you may notice the 'summer darkness'. The leaves of beech grow on a branch system that consists of overlapping series of flat planes which prevents light from reaching the forest floor.

Cross the Bird Bridge, but on the far side note the oak tree immediately on the left of the bridge. It is the first of a line of mainly mature oak trees running along the left of the right forking path. Counting these trees, cross the Viaduct Road and stop by the fifth or ninth one.

The trees in this line may be descendants of Whytebirche Wood that was standing here in the middle ages. When this woodland was cleared for farmland probably around 1600, it is possible that strips of trees were left to form the spine of enclosing hedges. This may be one of these hedgerows for the fifth and ninth trees are not oak but wild service, or 'chequer', trees. This species is an indicator of ancient woodland because it is extremely slow to colonise and then almost always by suckering. Today it is probably the least known of our native trees but in prehistoric times its fruit was a staple food. Its leaf is rather like a maple, and its brown berries, or 'chequers', used to be hung up on strings to 'blet', or ripen. Its taste is distinct – 'with hints of apricot, sultana, overripe damson and tamarind'. It was also the basis of a popular alcoholic drink, the name 'Chequers' being associated with a number of pubs in Kent and West Sussex.

The tenth and last tree in this line is a remarkable twisted and hollow beech. Look inside and feel its extraordinarily polished patina created by generations of children climbing inside it.

Turn right at 90 degrees and walk through the trees for 50 metres.

Around this area you will find a number of non-native trees, robinias and maples planted by the lord of the manor as part of his proposed villa development in the nineteenth century (see p. 136).

Turn left up the Viaduct Road, until you reach the open plateau known as the Upper Fairground on your right.

In 1798, when it was feared that Napoleon Bonaparte might invade, a volunteer corps called the 'Loyal Hampstead Association' was raised. It exercised on this plateau, which became known as the Battery.

Along the upper edge of this plateau is a row of large Lucombe oaks, a hybrid between the Turkey oak and the cork oak which occurs naturally in southern Europe. They were first raised from seed in England by Mr Lucombe, an Exeter gardener and nurseryman, in 1765. It is almost evergreen, hanging onto its leaves until the early spring. Do not be deceived into thinking this is an ancient hedgerow line. It is a nineteenth century ornamental planting by the lord of the manor.

Cross the Spaniards Road to return to Jack Straw's Castle.

The Heath

3.75 km / 1 hr

BEFORE YOU WALK

This walk takes you onto part of what remains of the common of the manor of Hampstead, an area that we know was referred to as 'the heath' from at least as early as the fourteenth century. It is worth doing the Geology Walk first and looking at the map of Hampstead manor on p.79.

Heathland – an open and more or less treeless landscape – occurs on well drained and acid soil, where heather, gorse, bracken and acid-loving grasses flourish. 'Lowland' heaths like the Heath (as opposed to upland moors) are ancient and wholly man made. Unless they are maintained, traditionally by grazing domestic livestock, they revert to scrub and woodland, as has now occurred over much of the Heath. The first lowland heaths developed in Mesolithic times, and became more widespread in the Neolithic and Bronze Ages as wildwood was cleared for agriculture and stock-rearing. Many of these lowland heaths became common land and, as such, became part of the formal land tenure concept of the manorial system.

Common rights over land had evolved before the Norman Conquest to complement the open-field system of strip cultivation. Members of the manor community enjoyed rights over the common such as to graze their cattle, gather fuel and, in the case of Hampstead Heath, to dig for sand. The Norman kings tried to regularise the system, but the precise extent of commoners rights versus the rights of the manorial lords was never given legal definition and for 800 years there were conflicts of interests. It is partly thanks to these ancient rights that we walk across the Heath today.

Many heaths were shared between two or more village settlements in Saxon times but became increasingly incorporated into a particular manor. These areas, less suitable for cultivation, were a vital part of the rural economy, providing pasture as well as gorse, bracken, heather and turf, materials for fuel, bedding and building. Small areas of heathland were often kept open in the middle of woodland, and this was almost certainly so in the case of the Kenwood estate in the middle ages, as mentioned in the de Blemont grant of 1226 (see p.70).

The number of heaths and commons began to diminish in the late seventeenth century, as agriculture became more intensive and specialised. In the case of the Heath, the expanding village ate into common land. As heaths diminished in importance in the rural economy, public perception of them also changed. They became increasingly viewed as barren and desolate wastes, inhabited by highwaymen and footpads (see p.34).

Real heathlands are now rare. Once there were many across northern Europe, but now there are few outside England. The Heath has some small patches of gorse and broom, and some areas of acid grassland. Scrub and woodland have encroached now that grazing has stopped, and neither heather nor bracken can withstand trampling by so many people.

Start: This walk, therefore, appropriately starts at Hampstead Heath station by South End Green, the initial source of the trampling.

But before setting out, cast an eye down to South End Green on your left. This was a hamlet called Pond Street in Tudor times. It was at the southern corner of the common and several fields away from Hampstead village centred on Frognal Rise. The pond which gave it its name was filled in and replaced by a green in the early nineteenth century, and subsequently by the bus terminus and public toilets. South End had become a fashionable place to live.

South End's gentility was shattered by the arrival of the railway in 1860, and then by horse-drawn trams six years later. Suddenly hordes of people particularly from the east end of London flocked to South End at week-ends and more particularly on bank holidays. The Heath was transformed by the arrival of sometimes up to 100,000 on a single day. An Easter fair, with barrows, tea gardens, games, dancing and donkey rides, attracted large numbers, and in its hey-day stretched virtually from South End to the Spaniards Road. Donkeys, as far as the prim residents were concerned, were harbingers of vulgarity. One of them complained to the Heath keeper, 'hoping [he] will do something Not to suffer the horses and Donkeys to stand so ner his premises...languige bad. Nusance great.'

Cross the bottom of South Hill Park, and enter the south west corner of the Heath under the canopy of towering plane trees.

This rather dreary entrance to the Heath was once the lowest of the Hampstead Ponds (see p.29), but it became polluted and was filled in 1892, and the limes and planes planted (see the photograph of the newly planted trees on p.30).

Follow the main path onto East Heath, and walk across the open grassland keeping the ponds on your right.

Dancing on East Heath, the Vale of Health Hotel in the background, c.1905:

'Oh!
Hampstead is the place to ruralize
Ri-ti-turalize, extra-muralize
Hampstead is the place to ruralize
On a summer's day.'
(Mid-19th century music hall song)

This is the south eastern part of the old common, its eastern
boundary being the old stream bed of Hampstead Brook later
excavated into a chain of ponds. It extended over West Heath, Sandy
Heath, East Heath and over the northern part of the present day
Hampstead village.

As you walk up the hill you will be crossing from London Clay
onto Claygate Beds, the sandier beds which overlie the clay. There is
no precise demarcation and the two materials are often mixed, as
you can tell from the varying textures of grass. Look carefully at the
changing grasses as you walk up the hill. The grasses on the higher

acid and sandy soils are finer leafed, harder in texture and less intensely green than the broad leafed grasses on the clay. In summer sheep's sorrel, with its tall rust red flowers, is found in abundance, but only on the sandier Claygate Beds and Bagshot Sand. Damp pockets of lusher grass and often buttercups, indicate the spring line between the London Clay and Claygate Beds.

This open area may not seem at first glance to be of great wildlife interest but natural grasslands are increasingly rare and are home to many invertebrates, most obviously butterflies.

Most British butterflies are associated with grasslands. Most species will collect nectar from a wide variety of plants but many will only lay their eggs on certain grasses, the food plant of their particular larvae. The grassland butterflies most likely seen in this area are the Meadow Brown, Gatekeeper, Skippers (Large, Small and Essex), and Small Copper.

Butterflies, incidentally, are themselves named after the Brimstone, common enough on the Heath and immediately distinguishable for its yellow 'butter' colour. They can often be seen on the Heath emerging from hibernation from early April, the females reconnoitring for suitable buckthorn.

Cross the main east-west route, the Boundary Path, close to East Heath Road. Pick up the main path to the Vale of Health Pond. After the Parent and Children's enclosure on your right, branch left off the main path, pause on the high ground above the Vale of Health Pond and turn to look across the pond towards Parliament Hill.

John Constable frequented and painted much of the Heath. After their marriage the Constables had settled in Charlotte Street. From 1819, during the summers, they took a house in Hampstead partly for Maria's health – she was consumptive – and also because John

*Looking south, across East Heath when still a treeless common. Lord Southampton's
Fitzroy House is visible on the slopes of Highgate at the far left.
(John Constable, c. 1822)*

found inspiration in the skies and views around the Heath. Here was
a natural observatory, and he was fascinated by the weather.

Constable must also have found life in London and Hampstead a
welcome distraction from the deepening agricultural depression
that was bringing great changes to his beloved Suffolk countryside.
He was a very conservative Tory in his attitude on rural affairs, but
by coming to Hampstead he did not escape unrest and controversy.
The first round in the battle for the Heath began a decade later, in
1829 when the lord of the manor submitted his first Private Bill to
Parliament with the intention of developing the Heath (Walk No. 9).
However, we do not know what Constable's views were on this.

Constable's Hampstead works are very different from the lush
pastoral landscapes of Dedham Vale on the Suffolk-Essex border.
On the Heath he was preoccupied by the more abstract, the shifting
effects of light and shade with wind and skudding clouds.

Branch Hill Pond: 'Sunshot clouds of a Showery Sky'
(John Constable, c. 1830)

When you reach the tarmac road to the Vale of Health, turn right and almost immediately left, onto a rough footpath up a bank which winds through a young mixed wood of sycamore, elm, bird cherry and rowan.

On your right is the Vale of Health hamlet, which grew from an early encroachment on the common, a single house and harness shop in the early eighteenth century. One Samuel Hatch, collarmaker, was granted a plot of land just above the swamp line, no doubt as an encouragement to move his probably malodorous business away from the highway where he had been dumping hides.

Continue walking around the Vale of Health 'bowl'.

You will see a little uphill on your left a brick enclosure, the last of a succession of village pounds, dated 1787, where stray or unauthorised animals were impounded. Illegal grazing was a constant problem. In 1835, for example, the keeper caught a Mr Veale (yes, truly his name) of Fortune Green, trying to pasture no fewer than fifty cows.

On the west side of the Vale of Health veer to your left to climb the steep bank past the gorse, then through a group of pine and robinia onto Spaniards Road.

Gorse, also known as furze or whin, was widespread over the old common and is one of the most characteristic plants of heathland with its bright yellow coconut-vanilla smelling flowers and seed pods that crack open noisily in the sun. It was highly valued, for its wood burnt fast, good either for kindling or for bread ovens. The young shoots were fed to livestock, the branches being first pounded and bruised to make them soft enough to eat. The Hampstead washerwomen, famous from Tudor times, spread their clean linen on the gorse bushes to dry, which gave the dried linen a fragrance of honey and coconut. Gorse was so useful that on many commons strict rules applied governing when and how much could be cut.

When you reach the Spaniards Road turn left and cross at the second zebra crossing which takes you to the path onto West Heath to the right of the Flagstaff.

The flagstaff is the site of a fire beacon, one of the network of beacons on high ground between the south coast and London that provided warning of the approaching Spanish Armada in August 1588.

Follow the path downhill, passing a glade on your right, until you come to a large open grassy area. Skirt around the right

side of this, then bear right towards the ponds and boggy area advertised by reeds and tussocks of purple moor grass.

Before it was drained in 1881 this bog was double the size and was deep enough for cows and horses to get seriously stuck. Botanically it made West Heath the most interesting part.

The Heath holds an important place in the history of botany, for being so close to the city it was a favourite and convenient place for London herbalists and apothecaries to collect their specimens. One of these was John Gerard, one of the earliest scientific collectors. Gerard was accused of plagiarism and inaccuracy, but he is remembered despite these failings as the author of *The Herball or General Historie of Plantes*, published in 1597: 'the most useful, fragrant and refreshing of all old time herbals ... and by far the most amusing.' He knew the Heath well and described some plants he found growing there: 'cotton grasse groweth upon bogy and such like moorish places, and it is seene upon the bogs in Hampstead heath.' He was very knowledgeable on old English herb lore and his book included some 'quaint conceits about the vertues of herbs', for example, sweet marjoram 'for those who are given to over-much sighing' and those 'as cannot brooke their meate, and to such as have a sowre squamish and watery stomache, as also against the swonning of the heart.' *The Herball* was enlarged and amended by another well known London apothecary and field botanist, Thomas Johnson, in 1633. Johnson, while admiring Gerard's work, could not resist pointing out all his faults, even accusing him of deliberately planting a wild peony which he claimed to have found by chance.

As a Hampstead doctor remarked in 1734:
> 'The Apothecaries Company very seldom miss coming to Hampstead every spring, and here have their Herbarising Feast; and I have heard them often say that they have found a

greater variety of curious and useful plants, near and about Hampstead, than in any other Place.'

In 1815 the young John Keats, after his apothecary apprenticeship, came to London to continue his medical studies at Guy's Hospital. His lecturer in medical botany was William Salisbury, a great believer in 'reading the book of nature', rather than sitting in a lecture hall. He led his students out on field trips to the meadows and woods around London, including Hampstead Heath. It is just possible that it was he who gave his name to Salisbury Plain, the field on which the Lido now stands. Here on the Heath they found tormentil, wood avens, bogbean, coltsfoot and lady's smock, all useful medicinal plants. It was undoubtedly on these herborising excursions that Keats came to know the essential character of his native herbs and flowers to which he gave such powerful expression in his poetry.

Most of the heathland plants listed by early botanists survived until the end of the nineteenth century, for example, ling and bell heather, bilberry, and needle whin. There were also wet-heath species like cross-leafed heather, common cotton grass, purple moor grass, round-leafed sun-dew, bogbean (used for curing rheumatism), marsh violet, royal fern, sphagnum mosses and creeping willow. Most of these have now disappeared because of drainage, the spread of woodland and human trampling, to which heather and bracken are particularly vulnerable, and also because at this same time the Heath ceased to be part of a wider countryside as rapid urbanisation isolated it. Remarkably, some species have survived, for example purple moor grass and creeping willow, and others may return since the bog is being made boggier again.

After circling the bog, retrace your steps back to the Spaniards Road. Take the main pathway (the Viaduct Road) to the right

off Spaniards Road just opposite the flank wall of Heath House. Follow the track for about 250m until you reach the path branching off to your right, leading down to the Vale of Health.

The flat area on your left, known as the Upper Fairground, was dug up to fill sandbags in the last war, and then filled in and levelled off with bomb rubble.

Follow the path down the hill to the Vale of Health. The boundary of the common runs along the line of the brick wall from the 'pepperpot' brick hut on your left. Continue on the path along the top of the embankment and take the first small footpath on your left just after the end of the pond by the redwood. After about 20m turn left at a large Turkey oak and make your way through the woodland with willows, birch and poplars down the slope towards the stream. Follow the downward course of the stream. Cross the Boundary Path and continue walking towards the group of crack willow and the small railed enclosure.

The crack willow is a native, often seen as a pollard along river banks. It is so named because the trunk grows so fast it often splits open, and perhaps also because the shoots snap off cleanly at the base with a sharp crack. They are well known for providing a haven for other plant species. Look carefully at the sprawling forms of these trees and you will see numerous other species living on them. This particular site is nationally important for mosses and lichens. Two mosses found here are virtually extinct elsewhere in eastern England. Lichens were once used for dyeing. In the middle ages several species were used as medicines, chiefly according to the relationship between their appearance and the disease, for example tree lungwort was used against lung disease, and the flat orange/ yellow lichen against jaundice.

Walk past the crack willows and several large poplars. Pick up the footpath which takes you along the west side of the mixed bathing pond. On your right is open grassland and on your left the woodland edge.

These transitional habitat zones, in this case between woodland and open grassland, are usually rich in wildlife, especially butterflies and hedgerow birds. Several bird species nest in bushes and trees but feed on open ground, and several butterflies, for example the Speckled Wood, Orange Tip and Gatekeeper, are often seen at the woodland edge but lay their eggs on plants of open ground. The Orange Tip larvae feed on wild mustard (to be found in many places on the Heath) and accumulate mustard oil in their bodies so as to be unpalatable to birds.

Continue on the footpath past the other two ponds back to South End Green.

An introduction to the two manor walks

The following two walks explore the 'manors' into which Kenwood and the Heath fell during the middle ages, for which a brief introduction may be helpful.

Were we able to see the area of Hampstead Heath as it was then, we would have found it unrecognisable. Middlesex was more heavily wooded than most counties and possibly a third of the environs of Hampstead Heath would have been woodland, no doubt with heathland clearings. Sandy, East and West Heath would probably have been largely heathland, grazed by a few sheep, goats and, where wooded, by a few pigs. We would have been astonished by how few people there were. This part of Middlesex was quite sparsely populated, with probably less than 10 persons per square mile. One might have walked the Heath and not met a soul. What little farming there was would have surprised us for the huge labour required for meagre rewards, and for its rudimentary technology.

In 1086 William the Conqueror authorised a major survey, known as Domesday since its investigative thoroughness suggested in the popular mind the rigour expected on the Day of Judgement. Domesday listed the manorial landholdings, reckonable productive area, labour resources and potential across most of England. The Norman manor was the basic unit of production and Domesday encourages a temptingly easy picture of each manor with its lord and its peasants and acreages neatly tabulated as if to suggest a consistent feudal system introduced by the victorious Normans.

In practice the term 'manor' means no more that a parcel of land, rather than implying there were manor houses everywhere inhabited by the magnate class. Manors usually possessed four types of land:

arable; pasture and meadow; woodland; and finally the 'waste' land. The waste might well be open heath, scrub, waterlogged tracts or woodland, or a combination of these. Two administrative categories of manorial land are of relevance: demesne land, worked for the benefit of the lord, and 'common' land used by the free and unfree tenants. One or two peasants might be free but most were not free to leave.

These peasants gave their lord quantified yearly labour service on the demesne land and shared the common land, some of which was good enough to grow their own crops and the rest – often called 'waste' – on which to graze animals, collect firewood, dig turfs for roofing or fuel, and possibly grow and cut underwood. Waste, often a large part of the manor, was a vital resource for peasant survival, its meaning quite different from today's. However, the common land remained in the ownership of the lord, and it was he who determined the rights of his tenants, and the extent of the common land. Over the years, with expansion of both the population and the economy, waste was progressively reclaimed as arable, pasture or managed woodland, often to the benefit of the lord and the detriment of the peasantry.

The system, although they applied it with greater rigour, largely predated the Normans. The estates of Hampstead and Tottenhall (into which Kenwood and Parliament Hill Fields fell) were both Saxon creations, in existence well before the Norman conquest. Most Norman manors overlaid such Saxon estates and formalised an existing class system, succinctly described half a century before the Conquest:

> 'The throne stands on these three supports: *laboratores, bellatores, oratores. Laboratores* are they who provide us with sustenance, ploughmen and husbandmen devoted to that alone. *Oratores* are they who intercede for us to God …

Bellatores are they who guard our boroughs and also our land ... .'

Thus, the labourers had to support the other two classes. Many manors were granted by the king to religious foundations as well as warlords, in order to ensure that they had the income on which they could operate. This was particularly true of the land lying close to London.

One final point should be made. As early as the Domesday survey itself, manors were often no longer single units. Many lords, including religious foundations, leased much of their land to smaller landholders, a practice that increased over the following centuries with much land eventually becoming alienated from the original holder.

Livestock grazing (Averil Hassall, from the Holkham Bible, c. 1330)

The medieval manor of Tottenhall

4.5 km / 1.5 hrs

BEFORE YOU WALK

Please read the introduction on p.60. This walk and the succeeding one for the manor of Hampstead both explore the two manorial estates into which most of the Heath was divided throughout the middle ages. The manor of Tottenhall, also known as Tottenham, was a very narrow strip of land, bounded in the north by the ridge running from the west side of the Dairy of Kenwood House eastwards to Athlone House (just before Highgate village) and then extending southwards in a narrow tongue to Tottenham Court Road tube station.

Sometime before the Norman Conquest this manor had been granted by Edward the Confessor to St Paul's Church, an endowment to ensure the upkeep of the activities, staff and fabric of the capital's principal religious foundation. The church of St Paul had been first established in London in

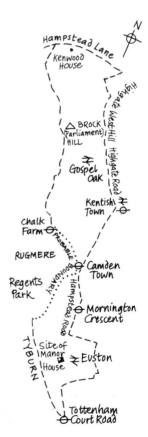

THE BOUNDARY OF
THE MANOR OF TOTTENHALL

604 AD, and by the end of the ninth century it already held a swathe of estates around London. Some were held by the Bishop of London himself, for example the manor of Hornsey on Tottenhall's northern boundary. Others, like Tottenhall were granted to the Canons of St Paul's.

Start: Kenwood House car park (see map on p.12). You will note a line of three plane trees running across the car park from the 'Out' sign towards an open lawn. Follow the path beside this lawn, passing the surviving portion of Kenwood

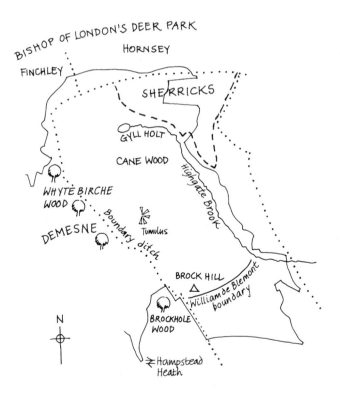

PART OF TOTTENHALL MANOR

Farmhouse on your right and the Dairy on your left. Walk down the gravel path with high banks on either side.

Ten paces before the gate you will note a hexagonal small stone boundary marker of 1845 in the ground on your left, just behind the fence. It marks the boundary of the parish of St Pancras and of the old manor of Tottenhall with the parish and manor of Hampstead. It is also the probable site of 'Bedegar's wood-clearing', mentioned in a Saxon charter of 986 as on the boundary of Hampstead. You are now entering the old manor of Tottenhall.

Enter West Meadow and take the main path. After 100m (more or less where a gravel path joins you from the left) veer off to the right towards the first large oak tree.

This is the first of a line of old oak trees on your right, marking the old boundary between Tottenhall and Hampstead manors (and between the parishes of St Pancras and Hampstead). You will find a large square boundary stone behind the second oak tree. Originally a ditch ran the whole length of this boundary, but stones were erected along this section when the Kenwood Estate incorporated part of the adjoining Evergreen Hill estate (see p. 116) in about 1845, when the ditch was filled in for aesthetic reasons.

Veer back towards the gravel path after the fifth (heavily leaning) oak tree.

From the sixth oak tree onwards you may note the boundary ditch just behind the oak trees, the original boundary between the two manors. You may also notice several old boundary oaks which have fallen by the ditch. As the gravel path curves sharply to the left you can see the ditch clearly very close to the path. This ditch was certainly in existence by the early thirteenth century but there is good reason to suppose that it may be much older. The Saxon charter of 986 AD for neighbouring Hampstead refers to a *haga*, or hedge, running along the manor's boundary with Tottenhall. One need not be too literal about the description of 'hedge' rather than a ditch since hedges, particularly where they marked an important boundary such as this, were very frequently integral with a bank and a ditch. As the intermittent parish boundary stones testify, long after manors ceased to be units of administration, it remained the administrative boundary between the parishes of St Pancras and Hampstead until they were amalgamated into the newly formed Borough of Camden in 1965, virtually a thousand years later. The ditch extends, with few breaks, as far as the corner of the South Hill Park gardens backing onto the Heath, on Parliament Hill.

Follow the ditch to Westfield gate. Go out of Westfield Gate, but veer right (see map on p.12). Almost immediately you will cross the ditch and once you have done so, turn left at the T-junction. Once again the path crosses the ditch, so that the ditch is again on your right. As soon as you can see the Hampstead Gate entrance to South Wood (about 30 metres away on your left), you will find a huge oak tree close to your right. The Hampstead and St Pancras boundary stones nestle in the boundary ditch behind it. Rather than continuing to follow the path itself past Hampstead Gate, veer slightly to the right as you cross the path which runs from Hampstead Gate down to the Bird Bridge in the gully on your right, and enter the beech grove. Keep the beech grove on your right side, and you should be able to find the ditch a little on your left quite easily, with its old oak trees (and one magnificent very large old beech). Although the ditch is no longer entirely continuous it should not be difficult to follow its course

southwards. (If you have difficulty, just follow the main path from Hampstead Gate down to South Hill Park/Parliament Hill. It shadows the ditch on its right pretty faithfully all the way.)

By the sixteenth century the northern end of Tottenhall manor was woodland for coppice and timber, which may have been very similar in species to today's South Wood, save for the present intrusion of rhododendron. Unfortunately, we know very little about its earlier history. Given the light, sandy and acidic soil, one may imagine that the landscape was largely one of woodland with heathy clearings, hinted at in the brief details of a land grant dated 1226.

If we are right in this conjecture, it formed part of much more expansive woodland straddling the boundary with Hampstead manor, where we know that 'Whytebirche Wood' covered much of the demesne land on the east side of Hampstead Brook (in other words all the land on your right down into the Hampstead Brook gully), approximately between the present Spaniards Road and South Hill Park. Another wood, Brockhole, stood on the slopes of South Hill Park itself and possibly spread over much of Parliament Hill.

Medieval communities depended on ready access to all three kinds of wood – faggots, underwood and timber. The Domesday survey, carried out in 1086, lists eight peasants as available for labour in the manor. Taking into account the families of these eight labourers, one may hazard a guess that there were probably not more than 50 people living on the entire estate at the time. Strolling across this land 900 years ago, you would probably have met no one.

No doubt the woodland was also used for hunting, particularly in the heyday of the chase at the end of the twelfth century. In theory the citizens of London held a cherished right to hunt in the woodland of Middlesex from pre-Conquest times. Henry I confirmed this right shortly before his death in 1135 but it is questionable how far the right was exercised except by those living on the manorial estate.

The woodland was also used as 'pannage', a designated grazing area for pigs. So it must have been reasonably endowed with oak and beech to provide the acorns and beech mast on which swine fed. According to Domesday it was able to support only a modest pig population compared, for example, with the thicker woodlands of Harrow, Hendon and probably even nearby Hornsey, possibly on account of its lighter sandy soils. The woodland would have been used by pigs belonging to the lord of the manor but he may have allowed its use as pannage by the peasantry of the estate as a form of remuneration for their labour service. Designated 'waste' would have been available as pannage to tenant labour as of right. One of their number would act as swineherd for all the pigs of the estate. Pigs were easily the most important and common form of livestock in the peasant economy. The lord might also keep sheep and goats, but cattle were still a rarer commodity.

Why did woodland survive into the sixteenth century at the northern end of Tottenhall? The northern end of Tottenhall, composed of Claygate Beds and Bagshot Sands, was easily the poorest for cultivation, a fact confirmed by a map of the period showing that the lowest yield woodland was on the highest ground at the northern end of the estate. The more fertile lower London Clays to the south (see the geological map on p. 15) had been cultivated probably for centuries. Another reason why the woodland lasted so long may be that it was still a profitable resource. By 1300 London had about 50,000 inhabitants requiring housing, fuel and the tools of various trades.

Continue following the ditch until you reach the Boundary Path running east-west across it.

The Boundary Path is the old track from Highgate to Hampstead. It is certainly more than two hundred years old and was probably the medieval route between the two villages. Quite how it acquired its name is a mystery, since it has never been a boundary.

On the far side of the Boundary Path, follow the north-south track as the ditch is lost on the escarpment for a few metres above the football playing field on the right.

The fact that this track faithfully follows the manor boundary all the way from West Meadow suggests that it may be very old. It may even be Saxon, like the boundary ditch itself. Another charter, dated 978 AD, speaks of a 'track' – in all probability little more than a footpath - down the eastern boundary of the manor of Hampstead. This may well be it, even if it is on the Tottenhall side of the boundary. It was probably used for the removal of timber from the estate and as a minor drove road in the middle ages. It may be difficult now to imagine it, but the track led down past the back gardens of Tanza Road, across Constantine and Fleet roads, then through woodland called Timberhurst, to a road on Haverstock Hill.

Keep following the track, keeping an eye on the ditch which disappears intermittently. Cross the east-west tarmac cycle track.

You will notice that you are now passing meadowland on your left. As you walk further south from South Wood, the land is increasingly open. These meadows south of the Tumulus have existed at least since the mid-sixteenth century.

Keep following the track and ditch until you reach the corner of South Hill Park's back gardens. Continue straight on, following the line of the back gardens. Forty paces after passing the Parliament Hill entrance onto the Heath, turn left onto a tarmac path.

After a few paces you will notice the remains of a ditch running along your left, in the undergrowth a few yards from the path. It marks the southern edge of what later became known as Kenwood estate, and is the remains of a boundary ditch dating back at least to the early thirteenth century. By this time this part of Tottenhall Manor had already passed from the Canons of St Paul's to a wealthy London landowner, William de Blemont. De Blemont also held lands just south of Tottenhall Manor, which became known by his name, 'Blemondsbury', today's Bloomsbury. His uncle had land in the City at Cornhill (the English version of Blemont). How long the de Blemonts had held this northern part of Tottenhall Manor is uncertain but William almost certainly inherited it from his father, and possibly his grandfather. In 1226 he granted his estate to one of the great London priories of the time, Holy Trinity, Aldgate, a grant confirmed by Henry III the following year:

> 'all wood, with heath, and all appurtenances as it is enclosed on all sides with ditches in the Parish of St Pancras of Kentisseton, next to the park of the Lord Bishop of London [Hornsey], towards the South.'

De Blemont made the estate over 'for the good of his soul and the souls of his ancestors and successors.' Holy Trinity was the beneficiary of many such gifts. Writing in his *Survey of London* at the end of the sixteenth century John Stow, the antiquary, remarks:

> 'this Priorie in processe of time became a very fayre and large church, rich in lands and ornaments, and passed all the Priories in the citie of London, or shire of Middlesex.'

Follow the path, keeping the ditch on your left side, ignore the path crossing from Parliament Hill and forking off to the right, but pause for a moment to consider the view of London in the middle ages.

By de Blemont's time London was still largely confined by its wall. The medieval cathedral of St Paul's would have been more obvious than its successor, for it boasted a spire of similar proportions to that of Salisbury, and stood close to the western edge of the city. The wall was probably visible from Parliament Hill, running across Ludgate Hill between the Cathedral and the river Fleet/Holebourne. The White Tower (of London) marked the south eastern extremity of the walled city, and would have been easily visible. The Priory of Holy Trinity Aldgate stood at the north east corner of the city. Only here, under Holy Trinity's jurisdiction, was there any serious expansion beyond the wall, into 'the Portsoken' a strip of land running down to the river by the White Tower. Several religious foundations also stood outside the walls. On the west side, apart from the New Temple (subsequently home of the law schools which became the Inns of Court), there were a few churches and foundations, some along the Strand: St Brides, St Clement Danes and Holy Innocents (St Mary le Strand); and others further to the north: St Andrew's Holborn, St Giles' Leper Hospital, St Martin-in-the-Fields and St James's Leper Hospital. Small settlements were beginning to grow close to some of these.

William FitzStephen's description of the city in the late twelfth century conjures up for us what lay between the city wall and Parliament Hill, and what we have lost:

'On all sides, beyond the houses, lie the gardens of the citizens that dwell in the suburbs, planted with trees, spacious and fair, adjoining one another. On the North lie pasture lands and a pleasant space of flat meadows,

London, Westminster and the Northern Heights, after Anthony van den Wyngaerde, c. 1543.

Although this view is from the south looking northwards, the Northern Heights dominate the centre of the skyline, and one can imagine the view southwards from Parliament Hill, just below the skyline. Looking at the picture one can see on the left, behind the Palace and Abbey of Westminster, St James's Leper Hospital (see the story of the Heath Extension, p. 142). In the centre middle ground, the large enclosure is

Convent Garden, with St Martin's Lane to its left running from Charing Cross to 'the broad military road' (Oxford Street and High Holborn). St Giles's can be seen behind Convent Garden. The river Fleet marks the western edge of the medieval city, which is dominated by St Paul's.

intersected by running waters, which turn revolving mill-wheels with merry din.'

By the mid-fourteenth century London proper had started to extend beyond its walls, as far as Holborn and Chancery Lane to the west, and about a quarter of a mile to the north. There was still some countryside between London and Westminister. However, Southwark on the south bank was now an established suburb, clustered around the religious house of St Mary Overie (Southwark Cathedral).

And now, back to today.

Continue walking, but 100m later fork left (towards St Anne's church spire) where another track from the summit of Parliament Hill crosses your path.

De Blemont's ditch is now on your right. Judging by the number of species, its associated hedgerow quite possibly dates back to de Blemont's time (see κ1 on p.97). As you descend the slope, you will note much of the lower hedge has been reconstituted.

Turn left along the side of the lowest of the Highgate Ponds, and turn right across the barrage separating it from the Men's Bathing Pond (the next pond up).

Before moving on, enjoy the great crested grebes here and on the Boating Pond. We are lucky to have them. In the late nineteenth century they were almost hunted to extinction, their skins for use as muffs, and their chestnut ruffs to ornament ladies' hats. Grebes avoid danger by diving. Hunters would pursue a grebe, discharging their guns to make it dive repeatedly, each time it surfaced. Ultimately, with the grebe utterly exhausted and short of breath, it did not require undue marksmanship (or sportsmanship) to polish it off.

Join Millfield Lane, turning left to walk up the hill.

Millfield Lane was probably the main road up to the Highgate Hampstead ridge in the middle ages. The indication of its antiquity lies further up the hill, but one may recognise that it is a less arduous route up to the northern heights since it follows the Highgate Brook valley to Hampstead Lane. The manorial boundary follows the line of Highgate West Hill, a stiffer and higher climb for haulage and therefore probably of later date.

Keep walking straight up Millfield Lane for 400m, ignoring the private road forking right to Fitzroy Park but taking the gravel track marked to Fitzroy Farm. After another 400m there is Heath on either side of the lane, and the right hand side of the lane is lined with oaks.

On your right are the slopes of 'Sherewick' or 'Sherricks'. De Blemont leased a twelve-acre plot lying next to 'the grove of Sirewic' to 'Safugle, son of Dering, and his heirs' in 1226. 'Sirewic' was an appropriate name for a south-west facing sun-trap, for in Old English it means 'bright settlement'. A century later, in 1325, Sherricks, both its wood and open land, was also made over to the Priory of Holy Trinity, Aldgate.

As you continue walking up Millfield Lane try to spot on your right a pair of wild service trees (see p.46) growing out of the bank, indicators of an ancient hedgerow or woodland.

Continue to the very top of Millfield Lane. Turn left at the gate leading onto Kenwood House terrace and immediately turn right. Pass Mansion Cottage on your left, and continue walking until the lane begins to curve to the right. Pause by the gas lamp and speed ramp.

Note on the right of the lane two parish boundary marks, a metal one for Hornsey and a stone one for St Pancras. They stand at the very end of the hedgebank of Millfield Lane (or Sherewick Lane as it was known until the sixteenth century), where it joins the line of old Hampstead Lane. Off to your right you will see the line of oaks marking the boundary and the edge of old Hampstead Lane before its realignment along its present course further north.

Take the first turning to the left and walk past the front entrance of Kenwood House, and follow the main carriageway back through North Wood to the car park.

North Wood was acquired on lease by the Kenwood estate in 1769 and integrated into the estate by changing the course of Hampstead Lane in 1793. It had previously belonged to the bishops of London, since before the Conquest, and formed the southern fringe of a famous deer park which was probably established in the early middle ages. The park fell mainly within the manor of Hornsey, but also straddled the boundary with the manor of Finchley to the west. Its western boundary ran along the back gardens of the houses fronting Wildwood Road (see p. 155), across Hampstead Garden Suburb to Lyttleton Playing Fields and thence eastwards to Fortis Green, and southwards down Muswell Hill Rd and Southwood Rd to the Gatehouse in Highgate village.

Parks containing fallow deer became fashionable in England in the twelfth century as status symbols for the rich and powerful. Their main purpose was to provide the owner with a supply of venison — a rare and great delicacy unavailable on the open market — and other game over the winter; they were not usually places where deer were hunted for sport, as was the case in the royal forests. In the fourteenth century the parker was permitted to keep his own livestock within the park confines, and this suggests that the park's primary purpose was the provision of venison. The bishop's lodge lay in the centre of the park in the centre of the present Highgate Golf Course.

The deer normally grazed over grassland and heathland where they did little damage, but woodland was usually fenced off because of the damage they caused to young tree growth. By the sixteenth century deer were no longer kept in the park. Hornsey Park was partly wooded, and also had some arable and pasture. A fragment of the boundary hedge or 'pale', once a deer-proof barrier, that enclosed the park still survives in Lyttleton Playing Fields, near East Finchley. The number of tree and shrub species in a sample length o' this hedgerow suggests it was planted in the mid-thirteenth century (see p.94). The name Highgate probably comes from Old English meaning a 'gate in the boundary hedge.' The southern boundary coincided with the old parish boundary.

5 *The medieval manor of Hampstead*

4 km / 1.5 hrs

BEFORE YOU WALK

The preceding walk traced the Tottenhall manor boundary falling within the confines of the Heath. This walk explores part of Hampstead manor's northern boundary, but also tries to picture the manor in the middle ages from the little evidence we have.

THE BOUNDARY OF
THE MANOR of HAMPSTEAD

It may be helpful at the outset to appreciate the overall size of the manor. We know approximately where its boundary ran from two Saxon charters of the late tenth century, the second of which, dated 986, granted the estate to the Abbey of St Peter, Westminster, which had been founded in 971. Hampstead was one of several estates awarded to the Abbey in a corridor of land running out from London to the north-west, no doubt to the detriment of St Paul's landholdings.

The Domesday entry tells us a little of what Hampstead manor was like at that time. Out of an estate of 1,900 acres, probably only about 250 acres of arable land were actually cultivated at any one time. The rest of the estate was a mixture of meadows, pasture, woodlands with the largest area probably being either heath, marsh or scrub 'wasteland'. The centre of the manor would have been the grange, from which the monks administered the estate. It stood near St John's parish church, at the junction of Frognal and Frognal Lane.

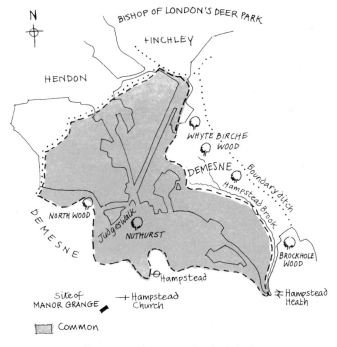

PART OF HAMPSTEAD MANOR,
COMMON and DEMESNE.

The labourers' dwellings would have been close by. The best fields of arable were probably on the sunny south and south-west facing slopes of the manor, straddling today's Fitzjohn's Avenue.

Domesday lists seven unfree men, a villein, five bordars (or boors), and one slave. They probably had about 60 acres of arable between them, of which half belonged to the villein, indicating his seniority in the grading of serfdom. Yet even he was liable to labour service. Since one third of arable land was normally rested each year, the villein probably cultivated 20 acres, on which subsistence is just possible, while the more lowly bordars would have had only 4 acres each, compelling them to give most of their labour to the demesne. They would have done most of the monks' work.

Start at Judges Walk (see the map on p.12). The nearest relatively easy parking is on West Heath Road and Branch Hill.

This walk begins with a post-medieval distraction. Judges' Walk is an old and diminished avenue, probably planted in the early eighteenth century. Originally it was a triple avenue with elms, beeches and chestnuts. It was known as Prospect Walk and its present name rests on the unsubstantiated story of London's judges fleeing to Hampstead from the Great Plague of 1665.

Prospect was an appropriate name, for until Branch Hill (to your left as you look out over West Heath) was built upon, in the nineteenth century, and West Heath became transformed from heathland to woodland in the twentieth century, the outlook must have been magnificent. As the poet Anna Letitia Barbauld, who came to live in Church Row, Hampstead in 1785, remarked 'the mall of the place, a kind of terrace, which they call Prospect Walk, commands a most extensive and varied view over Middlesex and Berkshire, in which is included, besides many inferior places, the majestic Windsor and lofty Harrow.' The precipitous slope down to

West Heath is the result of sand digging.

However, there is a more relevant purpose in starting here since, in spite of all the changes of the past 150 years, one can still see the lie of the land and try to imagine the scene in the middle ages.

A survey of the manor carried out in 1312 gives us an idea of where the woodland proper was, probably unchanged since Domesday. You are presently standing near the northern edge of 'Notehirst', or more probably 'Nuthurst', a wood extending back down the hill virtually to Hampstead tube station. Although it was part of the demesne land, the commoners (or tenants) were allowed to graze animals here throughout the year. We can guess both from the name and also from the statement that there was no pig-grazing, that it may have been a hazel wood and possibly coppiced. Hazel would have done well on the acidic Bagshot Sand. No doubt fences were erected around recently coppiced sections of the wood to protect new shoots till they had grown above the animal 'browse line'.

Look left across Branch Hill to the housing on the western edge of West Heath.

A larger wood, 'Northwood' stood here in 1300. It was probably predominantly oak. Tenants' grazing rights were allowed here throughout the year but there was no pannage.

Descend from Judges Walk, and make your way (across the final uphill leg of West Heath Road) towards the top of Platts Lane, about 750 metres away, keeping Branch Hill/West Heath Road within sight on your left. (If you feel uncertain of your way, descend to Branch Hill on your left, and turn right to walk along Branch Hill-West Heath Road until you reach the junction with Platts Lane.)

A popular race course stood on West Heath during the early part of the eighteenth century and it was here, as he recalled in his diary, that the itinerant preacher, George Whitefield, sought to save Hampstead souls in May 1739:

> 'The audience was of the politer sort, and I preached very near the horse course, which gave me occasion to speak home to their souls concerning the spiritual race. Most were attentive but some mocked.'

When you are opposite the top of Platts Lane, turn right along Sandy Road, the track leading northwards.

Sandy Road is clearly the continuation of Platt's Lane and runs just inside the northern boundary of the manor of Hampstead to North End. It was evidently the main access route to the northern parts of the estate, and one can imagine produce being carted down this track, via Platts Lane and West End Lane, to Watling Street (Edgware Road) and thence to London, to avoid the more direct route over the steep top of the Hampstead-Highgate ridge. (The Spaniards Road itself was probably only laid in the early eighteenth century, and the section of Sandy Road from North End across to the Spaniards only laid in the second half of the same century.)

The manorial boundary follows the line of the back-garden fences on your left, and if you care to investigate, you will see that this fencing is itself standing in a shallow ditch, presumably the medieval and possibly Saxon, boundary. To the north lay the manor of Hendon, though in Saxon times Hendon was divided into four estates. This part, running as far as the River Brent (bordering part of the North Circular) and its tributary Mutton Brook (bordering a further part of the North Circular and Falloden Way), was a separate Saxon estate called Bleccanham.

The whole of East, West and Sandy Heaths were probably

heathland at the time of Domesday, and it must be to this that the 1312 survey refers when it says, 'there is a certain heath, the heather [or brushwood] of which will fetch two shillings in average years.'

Pause at the second entrance to Golders Hill Park.

On your left you will notice again the clear remains of a hedgerow bank just inside the Park, indicating the edge of Hodford farm. Hodford farm, close to today's Golders Green tube station, was established as a sub-manor of Hendon in the thirteenth century, if not earlier, and was separate from the fourteenth century onwards. One may try to imagine a likely medieval landscape here of Hodford's harvested coppice and timber woodland and open fields to the left of Sandy Road, and Hampstead's sandy – and largely treeless – common on the right. From this second entrance to Golders Hill, the manor boundary doglegs around the northern side of the bandstand before making for the junction of North End Road and Hampstead Way. A couple of oak trees on the open lawn indicate where the old boundary bank once ran.

Continue up Sandy Road. At North End choose whether you wish

(i) **to follow as close to the manorial boundary as possible. If so, turn left into the tiny alley Heath Passage, cross North End Way and walk through Wildwood Grove (a slight dogleg to your left) and turn left along the track at the top of the steps, or**

(ii) **follow Sandy Road to North End Way and take a slight dogleg to your right into North End (on the right of the Old Bull and Bush), turn left at the first cross roads and follow the track to Wyldes.**

Wyldes Farm, which was probably built in the sixteenth century, stands just beyond the boundary (which runs through its front garden), in the manor of Hendon to the north, and is discussed in Walk No. 10.

Continue walking along the track running parallel to Wildwood Road.

This track, now called the Cooling Track, is probably a continuation of the manor boundary track we have followed from Platts Lane. The boundary itself is clearly marked by the ditch and bank on the left. This ditch has been maintained. Dry boundary ditches (like the Tottenhall-Hampstead boundary running across the Heath) could normally be left largely unmaintained since it took many years before they filled with leaves and debris. Those, however, that were also drains or streams had to be regularly scoured to prevent silting.

When you reach the end of the straight track follow it around to the right.

From here it is no longer possible to follow the boundary since it runs another 100 metres beyond the edge of the Heath before turning towards the Kenwood Dairy. The point where the boundary turns was known as Sandgate in Saxon times and is where the manors of Hendon, Hornsey and Hampstead met (Sandgate is discussed more fully on p.153). The Saxon charter of 986 reads: 'First from Sandgate, so eastwards to the wood-clearing of Bedegar.' Bedegar's clearing, no doubt where a man of this name lived, was probably very close to the Kenwood Dairy (where the Hampstead-Tottenhall boundary leaves the Finchley-Hornsey parish boundary, see p.65).

Continue up the side of Sandy Heath, up the steps to the Spaniards. Cross the Spaniards Road at the pedestrian crossing, and turn right in the direction of the Whitestone Pond for 150m until it is possible to veer off to the left and skirt around the Elms (see map on p.12).

Close by the Elms gate house was the site of Mother Huff's, a tea-house for about fifty years up to 1728 where, in her own words, 'cakes and cheesecakes and the best of entertainment were to be had.' It stood beside the track that ran from Parkgate (an entrance to the Bishop of London's park, now The Spaniards Inn) across what became the Upper Fairground, and skirted the north side of the swamp in Hatchett's Bottom (The Vale of Health) coming out near the Whitestone Pond. Thomas Barratt, whose *The Annals of Hampstead* appeared in 1912, sniffily described Mother Huff's as 'ostensibly a tea-house' to which 'visitors resorted to have their fortunes told; and the Hampstead sibyl, in addition to revealing the future of her patrons, was not averse from aiding them in their assignations.' Mother Huff abandoned the site in 1728, taking her fruity business, in the words of *Mist's Weekly Journal*, 'to North End at the Hoop and Bunch of Grapes' [in fact, almost certainly in Golders Green].

Pass the lodge on your left, follow around the perimeter of the unsightly communications aerial until you have gone 20 paces beyond, where the fence turns a right angle to the left, opposite some old hollies on a bank. A couple of paces on, as you are facing a pair of tall beeches, turn right along a path with oak trees growing on its left hand side. These oaks are the remnant of an old hedgerow along the edge of the field now known as 'Dr Joad's Hockey Pitch'.

On your left note a curiosity: two of the 'hedgerow' oaks growing intimately entwined with beeches. On your right note the hollies on the bank. The bank is a surviving remnant of the track on which carousing young hopefuls made their carefree way to Mother Huff's.

The track soon loses its definition, but follow the line of oak trees which veer off sharply to the left along the side of a gully which is the spring head for a stream.

You are in fact following the line that divided demesne land (on your left) from the common heathland on your right, a crucial boundary between what was to the benefit of the lord of the manor and what was for the commoners, or 'copyholders', until the whole area became public property in 1871. We cannot be sure how old this boundary line is, but since much waste was turned into pasture or arable to serve England's economic expansion in late twelfth and early thirteenth centuries, this may be the period when what might still have been common land on your left became demesne. In fact the rapid diminishment of common land in this period led to enactment of the Statute of Merton (1236), which allowed the manorial lord to enclose as demesne only that land not needed to support the tenants' livestock. As a means of protecting commoners' interests it was largely ineffective.

Come out onto and cross the Upper Fairground, veering slightly left. Cross the Viaduct Road and find the conical brick 'pepperpot' hut, and follow the line of oak trees beyond it, running behind and parallel with the brick ha-ha down into the gully below the Vale of Health Pond.

The boundary between demesne and common land follows these old hedgerow oaks into the gully.

Before getting lost in the undergrowth, climb up to your right onto the path on the embankment holding in the Vale of Health Pond. Walk to the end of the embankment and turn sharp left. After about 100m find a suitable point to look down to the stream running down this gully.

This stream, Hampstead Brook, running down to South End marked the rest of the boundary between the northern demesne bank and the southern commons one. The presence of one or two small wild service trees along Hampstead Brook suggests surviving traces of ancient woodland.

Bearing in mind that the land on both sides of Hampstead Brook changes from Bagshot Sand to Claygate Bed and thence to London Clay (Walk No.1) one might question why one side of the stream was set aside as demesne and the other as common land. Just as the best demesne land was on the south west facing slopes of the estate, so here, too, the Abbey retained the warmer sunnier side of the Fleet valley for itself and allocated the cooler side to the tenants.

In fact, probably until the sixteenth or seventeenth century, the demesne land on the north side of the brook remained uncultivated and largely wooded. Whytebirche Wood, for example, extended southwards from the Elms/Mount Tyndal at least as far as the Boundary Path, the track from Well Walk (Hampstead) to Merton Lane (Highgate), and must have merged with Cane Wood. Its name suggests the kind of trees that once grew there. It may at some stage have been partly cleared heathland recolonised by birches. By the fourteenth century, however, there was probably oak and beech present, since the 1312 survey states 'neither grazing nor pannage is allowed' implying that both were possible but forbidden.

It will be recalled from the Tottenhall manor walk, that further south, on the slopes of Parliament Hill and what is now South Hill Park, stood another wood, Brockhole, again where grazing and pannage were forbidden. Parliament Hill was still known as Brock Hill in the mid-eighteenth century. The name Brockhole, or -holt, is something of a mystery. It might mean 'badger wood', or 'brook wood' (a stream runs beside the garden wall at the back of South Hill Park to the Hampstead Ponds), or it might be a corruption of 'Throckholt', meaning a managed wood. Take your pick. The ground is mainly London Clay, and one can be more confident that Brockhole was predominantly oakwood.

Woodcutters, in the period before the Conquest.
(David Sullivan, based on a Saxon illustrated calendar in the British Library)

Yet further south another wood, Timberhurst, stood in the area between Fleet Road and Haverstock Hill. Its name tells us its probable primary function and that the trees, growing on clay, were almost certainly oaks. The wood had a Saxon name but stood on land belonging to a sub-manor with the Norman name of 'Bel-Assis' or 'well-situated', so well situated in fact that Belsize now has its very own tube station.

It is tempting to imagine these woods as neatly defined areas, standing alongside cornfields in an idealised and orderly countryside. Such a vision is almost certainly misleading and they were probably ill-defined, with areas of thinly wooded 'waste' or heath in between. Managed areas of woodland might be fenced or hedged where young shoots were still vulnerable to livestock, but elsewhere the land would probably be unenclosed. It was the herd's responsibility to ensure livestock did not meander off the waste into demesne woodland. Most of the valley between the common and demesne lands was probably boggy. Usually each manor stipulated how many animals each tenant, depending on their status, was allowed to keep on the common land, a practice known as 'stinting'. A tenant could exceed the 'stint' on the payment of a fine to the manorial court.

Retrace your steps up to the embankment, follow the path that leads around the left side of the pond and the hamlet.

The 1312 survey, two centuries after Domesday, gives us a picture of life on the manor. Most tenants still had to do labour service. Stephen Bartram, for example, who had a house and 15 acres still had to do at least 17 days service each year, including 'one day at the winter sowing', 'two days hoeing the lord's corn', 'a day carting the lord's manure' and 'five days haymaking in the lord's meadow.' In addition to 20 pence annual rent,

> 'he will supply one goose worth four pence on the feast of St Peter's Chains, and he will supply two fowls worth twopence each at Christmas, and five eggs worth a halfpenny at Easter.'

Andrew Attepond, who helped with the survey, held 18 acres but – poor fellow – 'he will render double the dues and services of the aforesaid Stephen Bertram.' Some of the names of the customary tenants reflect their vocation, John the Miller, William and John Wodeward, Lawrence the Forester, John the Ffoghler (fowler) and Nicholas the Herd.

By 1372 the number of tenants, mainly subsistence farmers, had increased to over sixty, an indication that following the Black Death (1348-9) which roughly halved the population, the labour shortage forced manor lords to lease more land to the peasantry. It also, incidentally, halted the reclamation of waste and in some cases led to arable being returned to woodland. By the early fifteenth century the Knights Hospitallers held the whole manor as tenants of the Abbey. Following the dissolution of the monasteries in the 1530s and 1540s, Edward VI gave the manor to one of his favourites, and it remained in private hands thereafter.

Make your way back up through the middle of the bowl in which the Vale of Health sits, to the Whitestone Pond.

If you have not already done the Heath Walk you may care to note on p.54 the details of the brick enclosure surrounded by young trees and undergrowth on your left as you make your way up across the bowl.

The hedgerows

BEFORE YOU WALK

Unlike the other walks in this book which are perhaps overly prescriptive, you are invited to design and follow your own route for this walk, along the hedgerows of Parliament Hill Fields and through the woodland of Hampstead manor demesne, or East Park, (see p.79) to discover the hidden pattern of fields and meadows, and to find the Heath's oldest trees. As a guide you have the 1866 edition of the 25" Ordnance Survey map, reproduced on pages 98-99. This wonderful map, made at the apogee of British map-making, shows individual trees along the old field boundaries. As you will see, a large number of these trees are still standing and must have been significant in the 1860s to have merited inclusion on the map. This walk does not include the Heath Extension hedgerows, for which see p.155.

Many of the hedgerows, especially those of Parliament Hill, are now barely recognisable as hedges. Their maintainence fell into abeyance over a century ago and they have grown into something more like woodland strips. Others have disappeared completely except for the wonderfully satisfying lines of ancient hedgerow trees. In some places a little detective work is needed to find the old hedge line, and you may have to search for the clues of bank and ditch, old stumps or tell-tale cluster of elm suckers. Virtually every hedgerow and field boundary offers its own rewards.

Before you set off, a general word on hedges may be helpful. Broadly speaking there are three categories, those that have been specially planted as hedges, those that were formed from strips of woodland left when the wood was cleared and finally those that have grown up more or less by default along the untilled and uncut edges of fields. They are an ancient part of our landscape, often mentioned in Anglo-Saxon charters and probably much older even than that. A tenth century charter, for example, mentions the hedge on the eastern boundary of the manor of Hampstead (see p.66). But the period most people associate with hedges is the time between 1750 and 1850 when a series of Enclosure Acts gave official permission and encouragement to landlords to enclose their land. Over this period something in the order of 200,000 miles of hedges were planted, almost all of common hawthorn or 'quickthorn' as it was called. In fact the word 'hawthorn' is itself a corruption of the Saxon *haga* thorn meaning hedge thorn, indicating its close and longstanding identity with hedging. This most useful hedging plant is quick growing, tough and thorny, forming stockproof barriers when 'plashed', or 'laid'. This was done by partly cutting through the main stems and laying them along the hedge at an angle, lashing them to stakes and interweaving with other branches.

PLASHING OR LAYING A HEDGE

Trees, either self-sown or planted, were common features of pre-Enclosure hedges. They were usually shredded or pollarded and, as such, were a valuable source of wood. It is difficult now to visualize a landscape in which almost all trees were working trees, not decorative ones. You will see that most of the old hedgerow oaks on the Heath have in the past been pollarded and this has given rise to their interesting forms and very individual characters.

NEWLY SHREDDED   A FEW YEARS LATER

Field patterns and therefore the hedges which enclosed them, over most of the country tended to remain unchanged for centuries. It has only been in the post war period of agricultural intensification that hedges have really started to disappear, and this loss has awakened interest in them as historic features and as a habitat for wild life – nesting sites, refuges and 'corridors' in an increasingly bland agricultural landscape.

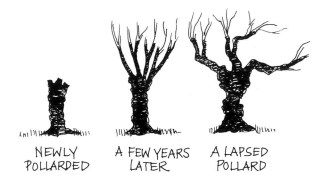

NEWLY POLLARDED   A FEW YEARS LATER   A LAPSED POLLARD

Hedges can of course be dated in a number of ways. Study has shown that the older the hedge the more plant species it usually contains, by colonisation rather than planting. Generally speaking, over a sample length of hedge, each species may represent about one century of existence, and you may care to count the species in some of the hedgerow lines on the Heath. Many such older hedges grew by default along field edges. Others are 'woodland ghosts', hedges that have survived the felling of ancient woodland which start their life as hedges with a number of species. More modern hedges, especially those of the Enclosure Act period, tended to be planted with a single species. Certain plants are indicators of antiquity, for example field maple, spindle and hazel which are slow to colonise.

The presence of the woodland, or midland, hawthorn or the wild service tree, both woodland species, indicate a hedge originally formed from a remaining strip of cleared woodland. The woodland hawthorn found in ancient woodland and old hedgerows is much rarer than the common hawthorn. It is not always easy to tell them apart, partly because they frequently hybridise and the leaves of both kinds are very variable. Generally the woodland variety has a much less divided leaf and usually two styles (and so two fruits) in each flower, while the common hawthorn has only one, and rarely two. It also comes into flower earlier than common hawthorn.

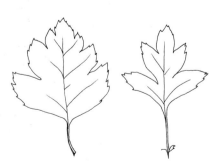

COMMON HAWTHORN LEAVES

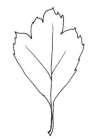

WOODLAND HAWTHORN LEAF

Evidence suggests that the area from Hampstead Lane down to and including the Tumulus field was coppiced woodland until about 1600. The fields south of this had probably been agricultural land for centuries. Hampstead manor demesne land later known as East Park (see map on p.137) also consisted of managed woodland until about the same time. Whytebirche Wood in the north (stretching over most of the demesne, or East Park), and Brockhole Wood in the south (on Parliament Hill).

A major change in the landscape took place in the century following the dissolution of the monasteries in the 1530s when these lands passed from the religious foundations of Westminster, St Paul's and Holy Trinity, Aldgate (see p.70). The new class of gentry landholders probably responded more quickly to economic change than the religious foundations would have done. In that sense the dissolution itself possibly hastened a process that would have happened anyway. Parliament Hill Fields were already open pasture by 1543 when they were formed as an estate separate from the woodlands to the north. That same year an Act of Parliament was passed to compel owners to maintain woods in the public interest. Complaints had already been made in many parts of the country regarding the loss of timber and underwood which deprived the poorer inhabitants of fuel and possibly grazing. The Hampstead area was just such an example. In 1556 a gentleman grazier, John Slannyng, cut down 20 acres of trees 'in a wood called Cayne Wood' and turned his 'horses, mares and cattle' on to it, destroying the new saplings. Slannyng, it was claimed, had cut down 14 acres of wood two years earlier 'in a wood called Wyldes Wood' [on the Heath Extension, see p.154] and 'had put his cattle in'. He had also kept 140 acres of Hampstead and another 120 acres in Chawcotts (Chalk Farm) 'in pasture rather than tillage', letting the land 'to butchers and inn-holders of London.' Hampstead's new manor lord,

Sir Thomas Wroth, had been acting similarly. He had 'sowlde the woodes growing upon the common of Hampstead without the goodwill and consent of the tenantes, conteyning by estimacion XL [40] acres', whereas 'ther shuld have byn cutt downe but the fowrth parte of the first yere, and the same to be enclossed.'

Woodfelling was a response to the change in economic climate driven by population growth. England and Wales increased in population from 2.2 million in 1525 to over 4 million by 1600. This increase was felt mainly in London itself. The capital's population, which was probably about 50,000 by 1500, grew to 200,000 by 1600 and almost 400,000 by 1650, nearly 10 per cent of the entire English population. By 1700 London contained twenty times more inhabitants than the next largest English city, Bristol.

London's population needs changed the topography of the Heath. Dairy pasture and hay meadows close to the capital rapidly commanded high prices. So did grazing and fodder for the resident horses and the huge amount of livestock driven into the capital for daily slaughter. These growing demands were probably the dominant factor that explains the loss of woodland and the meadow hedgerows standing today. To give some idea of the eventual scale we are speaking of, by the end of the eighteenth century it was said that no fewer than 10,000 animals were driven down Holloway Road and Upper Street Islington daily. It must have done wonders for local marrow growers, until the steam train put a rapid end to droving and free manure. By that time London also had a resident population of at least 10,000 horses, so the demand for hay was enormous. A secondary factor was the displacement of wood by coal as the more efficient if more polluting fuel. This too was largely a response to population increase. In 1560 London consumed 33,000 tons of Newcastle coal. By 1600 it was using five times as much. As fuel, the underwood of the Heath – Cane Wood, Gyll Holt,

Whytebirche and Brockhole – simply could not compete.

It is hoped that this short introduction will help you interpret what you find on your hedgerow exploration. The hedges are numbered and marked on the OS map overleaf and points of interest for most hedgerow lines are given below, but the listing is far from exhaustive, since there is a wealth of things to be discovered among the twisted old thorns and pollard oaks:

THE HEDGES OF PARLIAMENT HILL FIELDS

We have omitted the landscape at the southern foot of Parliament Hill, yet it is worth noting that even the humble hedgerow and bank on the east side of the Lido field, which when still countryside was known as Salisbury Plain, running behind the houses and William Ellis School were certainly there in 1800 and may well have been established in the sixteenth century.

We have listed the species we noticed in hedgerows K1 and K2 as an indication of the variety some of these hedgerows have on offer.

K1   This was the southern boundary of the estate of The Priory of the Holy Trinity, Aldgate from 1226, and continued to be the boundary of the Kenwood estate until Lord Mansfield extended his property down to where Mansfield Road now runs, in the early nineteenth century. There are several indicators of its great age:
- ditch and bank still visible along some stretches
- field maple present, usually found only in ancient hedges or in very modern planted hedges that consciously seek to use a mixture of native species.
- very old hawthorn stumps on the bank, some of which are woodland or hybrid hawthorns.
- here, as in several hedgerows on the Heath, you will find

OS Map 25″ to 1 mile (reduced), surveyed 1866.

elm suckers. It was highly competitive in hedges before the 1970s destruction through Dutch elm disease, and tended to suppress other species. Therefore hedges with elm may be much older than the number of species would indicate. You may be fortunate enough to catch sight of the White Letter Hairstreak butterfly as elm is its larval food plant.

You should have no difficulty finding hazel, oak, bramble, elm, alder, field maple, ash, hornbeam along this hedgerow. But beware the eastern section in terms of dating the hedge according to the number of species. This has been restored with newly planted hedgerow plants: spindle, dog rose, dogwood, hazel, rowan, hawthorn and ash.

K2 Documentary and species evidence suggests that this is an ancient (i.e. pre-1600) field boundary. Species found include the woodland or hybrid hawthorn, hazel, hornbeam, field maple, cherry, hornbeam, dog rose, ash and pollard oaks.

K3 The western half of this hedgerow was the boundary between the two parts of the estate when it was divided in 1525. At that time the northern part of the estate was still woodland.

K4 Only five oaks remain of this hedgerow to the east of the Tumulus. It was still a field boundary in 1804.

K5 This is a very rewarding hedgerow line to follow, with bank, ditch, and many ancient pollards and several old woodland and hybrid hawthorns.

K6 This is the eastern boundary of the two Diana fields (see p.118). Only the oaks survive from this hedgerow, but you can still pick out the gentle depression of the ditch.

K7 Only the pollard oaks survive from this hedgerow, running along the main path to the south east entrance to South Wood.

THE HEDGES OF HAMPSTEAD DEMESNE (EAST PARK)

| H1 | The hedge bank is still visible, with one surviving hedge oak. |

H1 The hedge bank is still visible, with one surviving hedge oak.

H2 This is the boundary between the manors of Hampstead and Tottenhall (see p.66) which probably dates back to Saxon times. Along much of its length the bank and ditch are clearly visible. There are intermittent old oaks and other trees along the hedge line on top of the bank. Look out for the old alder buckthorn close to the Boundary Path, which is the food plant for the Brimstone butterfly.

H3 This hedge line contains three surviving large oaks.

H4 This has only two extant hedge oaks, but it is quite difficult to tell which are the hedgerow oaks, and the footpaths do not help. One large oak is perched on a steep slope in the field north of this hedge line which has survived the digging of brick clay around its roots (on brickmaking, see p.139).

H5 Surprisingly, since this was a brick field, this hedge line has six surviving oaks.

H6 No trees survive on this line although the bank and ditch can still be seen.

H7 The Boundary Path has about seven surviving oaks alongside the LCC-planted lime trees of the avenue.

H8 Only two trees survive from this hedgerow. All evidence of the southern part has completely gone, destroyed by the digging for brick clay. Even after 130 years the area still looks disturbed, and the vegetation is typical of disturbed ground.

H9 This field boundary ran from the manorial boundary to the Bird Bridge. Four oaks survive.

H10 Six oaks may be found along the streamline to the Bird Bridge. It is a good place to see the chalybeate water (see p.21). Several young wild service trees may also be spotted.

H11   This hedgerow ran from the Bird Bridge, over the Viaduct Road up a slope and across a plateau. There are some very interesting trees: counting from the Bird Bridge, the fifth and ninth are handsome examples of the wild service tree (see p.46). The line ends with three quite small and twisted oaks.

H12   Pause at the top and try to imagine yourself in the hay meadow of 1800. From H11 walking downhill you come across a remarkably complete line of trees, two of which are dead but still standing, and another is a wild service tree.

H13   This is the Hampstead Brook hedgerow. Very few old trees have survived along this now wooded valley. A woodland hawthorn, or hybrid, and several wild service trees indicate a long history of woodland or hedgerow.

H14   This boundary of the demesne land still has 14 hedgerow oaks.

H15   The section on the Upper Fairground is not an old hedgerow but a line of Lucombe oaks, planted in the nineteenth century (see p.47). The old hedgerow extends from this line down the hill. The bank and ditch are still clearly visible. Several old oaks may be found, as well as other hedgerow species including a very tall hawthorn, sycamore, holly and elm suckers around an old stump.

H16   These are trees along the old track from Mother Huff's to the Vale of Health. Many of them do not seem to have been pollarded. The last tree of the line must be one of the grandest sessile (see p.43) oaks on the Heath.

H17   There are several oaks surviving along the edge of Dr Joad's Hockey Pitch before the line disappears into the gloomy laurel land of the Elms.

H18   H19   Several great oaks lead down into the gully, and then up again to meet the Tottenhall (Kenwood) boundary.

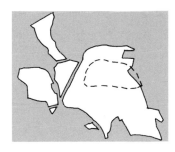

Houses and Landscapes of the Northern Heights: Fitzroy Park to the Elms

4 km / 1.25 hours

BEFORE YOU WALK

This walk explores the three eighteenth century landscaped estates on the southern slopes of the Northern Heights: Lord Southampton's Fitzroy Park; The Earl of Mansfield's Kenwood and Lord Erskine's Evergreen Hill.

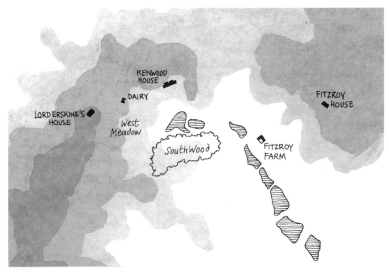

THE THREE LANDSCAPED ESTATES BETWEEN HAMPSTEAD and HIGHGATE C.1800

At the time of their creation the land was much less densely wooded than it is today, and the three landscapes were linked visually in a way now difficult to appreciate without the help of contemporary illustrations.

The eighteenth century saw a revolution in garden design. Gradually the prevailing fashion for symmetry, enclosure and formalism gave way to sweeping lawns and pastoral landscapes. It was, as Horace Walpole said, as if landscape designers 'looked over the garden wall and saw that all nature was a garden.' It was a mark of culture and social standing to design according to the prevailing fashion, and so from the grandest country seat to the most modest suburban villa, gardens were remodelled in the new style.

Consequently, Southampton, Mansfield and Erskine exploited what was already in the landscape, the water, woods, valleys and also the distant fields and views beyond their own estate boundaries.

Humphry Repton, the leading landscape designer at the end of the century, had a hand in all three estates. Unlike 'Capability' Brown, Repton was not a contractor and rarely supervised works. Essentially he provided advice, in the case of his more important commissions in the form of his famous trademark, a 'Red Book', so called because of its red morocco binding. The Red Book provided descriptions and suggestions and also watercolours showing 'before' and 'after' views intended to beguile his clients with his proposals. The actual construction of the landscape was left to the individual owner and one may assume that few schemes were executed exactly as Repton had advised. Of the three estates only Kenwood has a Red Book, and we know from this that many of his suggestions were indeed carried out, although he was not consulted as closely on the changes as he would have liked. At Fitzroy Park and Evergreen Hill his advice was possibly presented less formally.

Start at the southern end of Fitzroy Park (marked 'Private Road') at the junction of Merton Lane and Millfield Lane. Walk northwards (towards Highgate) on Fitzroy Park for about 200m. This road, incidentally, offers interesting examples of almost every decade of twentieth century domestic architecture. As the road turns sharply to the right, carry straight on along a paved road with houses on your left and allotment gardens on your right.

You are now in what was Fitzroy Park at the end of the eighteenth century. Fitzroy farmhouse stood behind the row of houses that you have just passed on your left. The farm fields themselves extended southwards in the narrow strip of land between Millfield Lane and Highgate West Hill.

The allotment land on your right was part of the eighteenth century Fitzroy Park. It was subsequently bought along with a large part of the Park by Lord Mansfield in 1840, to protect Kenwood's eastern flank from encroaching development. (Threatened again with development it was acquired within the campaign to save Kenwood in 1922 (see p.146), and sub-sold to St Pancras Borough with a restriction on building.) Don't imagine it is easy to get one of these highly desirable allotments. It takes five years on the waiting list. Moreover, you should consider the gender implications: women constitute only 12 per cent of allotment holders in the country as a whole, but comprise no less than 67 per cent in progressive Camden.

Continue following the footpath which carries on from the end of the road. After about 50 paces beyond the gate take the left branch of the footpath and pause close to the first large oak on the right of the path. Look down the slope towards South Wood.

Fitzroy House, Lord Southampton's villa, 1792.

The parkland spread more or less over the old medieval farm of
Sherrick's, the triangular wedge of land with Millfield Lane on the
west and Hampstead Lane to the north. Fitzroy House itself stood
near the top of the hill behind you, just about where Beechwood
(designed c. 1839 by George Basevi, achitect of the Fitzwilliam
Museum, Cambridge) now stands and since this is private, we are
denied the chance to imagine the view from the site of the house. The
field slopes down in a south westerly direction, the direction the
house itself faced. The landscape at the time was open, dotted with a
few clumps of parkland trees. To the west and south west one would
have looked across to Kenwood, with an unimpeded view of the
pasture lands of South Meadow, the Tumulus, and Parliament Hill
across the upper Highgate Ponds. Today one can only just see the
spire of the nineteenth century Christ Church in Hampstead above

the trees of South Meadow, but the Highgate ponds are no longer visible.

Lord Southampton was a shrewd eighteenth century developer. As Colonel Charles Fitzroy (he was great grandson of an illegitimate son of Charles II – hence the name Fitzroy) he had inherited the lease of what still remained of Tottenhall Manor. By Act of Parliament in 1768 he cleverly succeeded in acquiring the manorial freehold from the Canons of St. Paul's, giving him an enormously valuable estate which extended from Charlotte Street to Highgate. He built his villa in about 1770 on the demesne land in the north part of the manor, close to the old site of Sherrick's farmstead. The land around the house was landscaped, possibly by Brown, and the farmland, described as a *ferme ornée*, was run as a dairy farm, at that time a fashionable pastime for high-born ladies. Ladies Southampton and Mansfield vied with each other over the reputation of their respective dairy herds. Writing to her brother, the poet and Hampstead resident, Mrs Barbauld, duly passed on the current gossip:

> 'Lady Mansfield and Lady Southampton, I am told, are both admirable dairywomen, and so jealous of each other's fame in that particular, that they have had many heart-burnings, and have, once or twice, been very near a serious falling out over the dispute which of them could make the greatest quantity of butter from such a number of cows.'

The *ferme ornée*, where farm and fields were fashioned as a visual pleasure, was introduced into the English landscape movement early in the eighteenth century. Buildings were made more attractive, hedges planted with ornamental species and muddy tracks turned into gravel walks and carriage drives.

In the 1790s the house was remodelled by Henry Holland, better known for his design commissioned by Richard Sheridan for the

Theatre Royal, Drury Lane and also for Battersea Bridge. Repton was called in at about the same time to advise on the landscape. Why did Lord Southampton, as Fitzroy had now become, wish to alter a relatively modern country seat? It may have been to keep up with the latest fashion, but it may have been to accommodate his extensive family of nine sons and seven daughters. Repton may have introduced an element of formality to separate the house from the parkland. He preferred there to be a distinction between ornamental park and agricultural land. Nor did he think it right to have cattle, sheep or deer grazing right up to the walls of the house as Brown probably intended. Frustratingly, all this must remain conjecture. No evidence survives of either Holland's or Repton's endeavours, and neither house nor park survived for long. Lord Southampton died in 1797, the house was demolished in about 1828 and the estate was broken up soon after.

Before you move on, note one tiny surviving vestige of Fitzroy's parkland in the group of three trees in the middle of the field, a lime, a sycamore and a beech. It is anyone's guess whether Brown or Repton or, indeed, merely the estate gardener originally suggested planting them.

Continue to follow the footpath which passes close to the boundary fence of Athlone House (formerly Caen Wood Towers built c.1871 on what had been Fitzroy Park), along the upper edge of the field and down the slope to the ditch and old hedge line. If you are feeling agile you can weave your way down the slope along the bed of the ditch, choosing your way through a network of paths, over old tree trunks to emerge onto Millfield lane by the Goodison Fountain. Otherwise you can walk down either side of the hedgerow.

This, incidentally, is an ancient ditch with some hedgerow oaks dating back at least to the sixteenth century when these fields were part of Sherrick's Farm.

The fields either side of it, once Sherricks, then part of Fitzroy Park, were part of the land bought by the Fourth Earl of Mansfield in 1840 to protect Kenwood's eastern flank from development. Millfield Lane was previously the boundary between Fitzroy Park and Kenwood.

The fountain is in memory of Henry Goodison, Treasurer of the Kenwood Preservation Council (see p.146). Note the tell-tale orange stain of the iron oxide leached from the Bagshot Sands above.

Follow Millfield Lane uphill and turn left into the Pasture Ground through the second gate (the first is usually locked) on the left.

Repton was also approached by Second Earl of Mansfield, nephew and heir of the 1st Earl. What he saw when he first visited Kenwood in 1793 was a house remodelled in the 1760s and 1770s by Robert Adam, the Scottish neo-classicist who at that time was the most fashionable architect in London. Adam had worked for 15 years for the First Earl, extending and redesigning what was an unpretentious red brick mansion into a seat worthy of the Lord Chief Justice. All his furniture, pictures and books were to be moved from his house in Bloomsbury Square. But in 1780, just after Adam had completed his work, London erupted in a week of violence and destruction with the anti-Catholic Gordon Riots. Lord Mansfield, regarded as too pro-Catholic, was a prime target for the mob's fury and the rioters made for Bloomsbury Square where, in Dickens' description some sixty years later,

> 'They then began to demolish the house with great fury, and setting fire to it in several parts, involved in a common ruin

the whole of the costly furniture, plate and jewels, a beautiful gallery of pictures, the rarest collection of manuscripts ever possessed by any one private person in the world, and worse than all because nothing could replace this loss, the great Law Library ... .'

(*Barnaby Rudge*, 1841)

About sixty rioters then set out for Kenwood intent on further destruction. However, liberal quantities of ale supplied by the landlord of the Spaniards Inn and Lord Mansfield's own steward at the very entrance to the house delayed their progress until troopers from the 16th Light Dragoons arrived and sent them packing.

By 1793, the house sat on its terrace which extended in a lime avenue beyond the west end of the house along what was then the side of the kitchen garden. The lawn, or Pleasure Ground, which ran from the terrace down to the ponds was enclosed with a wall and belts of shrubbery. The front portico on the north opened onto an enclosed forecourt and then immediately onto the main road to Highgate.

Repton saw his task as transforming Kenwood 'which had hitherto been considered a mere villa' into a property which gave the impression of a country residence of elegance and importance. Certainly not everything that Repton suggested was carried out, but many changes followed his general ideas: additional rooms for the house, the extension of the terrace to the east, the building of new offices and kitchen buildings behind the extended terrace, the opening up of the Pleasure Ground into a sweeping lawn, the transformation of the kitchen garden into a flower garden and removal of the clutter of walls and buildings to the north. The re-alignment of the main road away from the front, and the design of two new entrance drives seem to have followed Repton's ideas closely. In many of his commissions Repton paid great attention to lodges which he felt set the scene, preparing the visitor for the style and grandeur of a mansion. He failed to persuade Mansfield to create a new 'and handsome approach' from the south. His sketch shows the road crossing the valley between the two upper Highgate ponds and sweeping around the edge of South Wood and up to the front of the house. He felt that the south facade with its 'magnificent terrace' was not seen with the advantage its deserved, and that the sham bridge was 'a deception unworthy of Kenwood.'

Continue up the path towards the house and then walk onto the lawn and pause just under the large old beech. This is a good place to look at the house in its setting.

The house sits rather severely on its terrace commanding rather than nestling into its landscape. That sort of division between house and grounds would have pleased Repton. He liked a degree of formality around the house to distinguish it from surrounding parkland.

Follow the path up to the house and walk along the terrace until you reach the mid-point in front of the house.

At the end of the eighteenth century there was a clear view, past the east of South Wood to the Highgate Ponds and all the way down to the city. Robert Adam said he could see ships passing up and down the Thames. Repton suggested screening out the houses of Kentish Town 'to create the illusion that Kenwood extended almost to the city of London.'

Today you can just see the top of the NatWest Tower, and if you move along till you are standing in front of the centre of the Orangery, you may see the Caledonian Clock Tower, and the North Downs beyond London.

VIEW from the TERRACE at KENWOOD.   *Seat of Earl Mansfield.*

Repton's proposed view from the terrace, with trees cut back from South Wood to reveal St Paul's and 'the waters with very little assistance of Art might be rendered apparently connected.'

Continue along the terrace to the lime avenue.

The lime *(Tilia vulgaris 'Pallida')* avenue was planted in about 1725. The condition of this avenue today perfectly illustrates the difficulty of restoration. When you begin to lose trees should you cut the whole lot down and start again to retain uniformity of size and age or only replace them when they die? This avenue was partly felled and replanted in 1961. More fell in the 1987 storm and were replaced. One or two of the original trees, or suckers of them, survive at the west end.

Turn right off the path just after the bend and walk through the wooded hollow of holly, rowan, birch and rhododendron until you reach the tarmac path. Turn left and after about 100 paces take the right fork, signposted 'Way Out' and leading to the car park.

The large oaks mark the line of the old main road which was moved northwards by the 2nd Earl, away from his front door. On your left, just at the fork in the path, the sunken line of the old road is quite clear.

The common rhododendron, native to the British Isles before the last glaciation, was re-introduced from the East in the nineteenth century. Acid loving, they do well on the Bagshot Sands and too well in some areas of ancient woodland and over many parts of western Britain, where they take over at the expense of almost all other species.

From the car park branch left towards Kenwood Farm.

Eighteenth century landscapes were designed to be explored and at Kenwood Repton wanted to create rich internal scenery 'with variety, incident and surprise.' He offered no specific layout in his Red Book, but his general ideas were followed. Winding paths led to all parts, boundaries were screened and views carefully framed to give the impression of a large estate. There were views down to the ponds and southwards over the open felds.

The present building is part of the octagonal farmhouse built along with the Swiss chalet-style dairy buildings at the end of the eighteenth century as a picturesque grouping. The outline of the farmhouse is marked by the low brick wall in the lawn. A large part of the Kenwood estate had been farmland, pasture mainly for dairy cows and hay meadows, from about 1600 when much of the woodland had been felled.

When Repton appeared on the scene the farm buildings were on the west side of the house near what was the kitchen garden and he proposed moving the farm to its present position further west and overlooking the dairy pasture. The new buildings were designed by George Saunders, architect for the extensions to the house and kitchen wing and, incidentally, the extensions for the British Museum. The Mansfields were caught up in the eighteenth century enthusiasm for agriculture. Purpose-built farm buildings demonstrated both wealth and modernity. It was common for the dairy buildings to be the most decorative part of the farm. They were thought of as 'polite' buildings, the province of the lady of the house and her daughters.

Follow the path which leads down to the left between the steep banks. As you pass through the gate turn sharp left and walk around the trees until you can stand in front of the Dairy.

The Dairy was designed with attention to hygiene as well as to its picturesque qualities. To keep the milk parlour cool an ice house was constructed directly underground. Chilled water was pumped up to a marble basin in the middle of the room.

From here you can easily imagine the pastoral scene: long views down the slope to the Kenwood lakes, and across the fields of grazing cattle. The cattle, a small herd of Warwickshire Longhorns, were hardly the most prolific milk producers but were considered the best looking 'in a gentleman's park.' They were usually milked by the milk maids in their pastures.

By the late 1770s, before the new dairy was built, the dairy was responsibility of a beautiful black girl, Dido Elizabeth Belle, daughter of Lord Mansfield's naval nephew and a black woman, presumably a slave, captured from a Spanish ship. Nothing is known of her fate, but the little girl was brought up at Kenwood and grew up under the care of the Mansfields, who had no children of their own but became guardians not only to Dido but also another great niece, Lady Elizabeth Murray, whose mother had died when she was a baby.

The cousins growing up together at Kenwood, the Sham Bridge and St Paul's in the background. Dido's exotic and rather theatrical dress, typical of the dress of many black people in eighteenth century portraits, indicates a lower social position to that of her cousin. But she was certainly not treated as a servant. Lady Elizabeth's gesture is one of affection, drawing her into the picture as a friend. Dido's cheerful smile and her finger pointing to her cheek, perhaps a way of drawing attention to her colour, gives us the impression of a lively and confident personality. (Attributed to Johann Zoffany, c.1780)

In 1772 Mansfield made an historic judgement in the case of a runaway slave:

> 'The state of slavery ......is so odious that nothing can be suffered to support it, but positive law. Whatever inconvenience, therefore, may follow this decision, I cannot say this case is allowed or approved by the law of England; and therefore, the black must be discharged.'

Dido was about seven years old at the time and it is difficult to believe that Mansfield was not influenced in his ruling by his undeniable affection for Dido.

Sadly we know nothing of Dido's life after Kenwood. Lady Elizabeth married and moved away, and Dido was well provided for in the wills of her father and great uncle. In 1794 she changed her name to Davinier, possibly marrying a clergyman of that name.

Retrace your steps to the gate, cross the main path across West Meadow and follow the small woodland path on the slopes of Mount Tyndal.

You can hear the traffic passing through the narrow tollgate by the Spaniards. Lord Erskine's house, was beside the Spaniards Inn while his garden was the other side of the road where you are now walking. A tunnel, now blocked, connected the two.

The house had originally been built illegally on the Heath in about 1680. It was bought in 1795 by Thomas Erskine, who later became Attorney General and Lord High Chancellor. Over the years Erskine acquired parcels of land to add to his garden, grants of the Heath as well as some demesne land, leases on the Shakespeare's Head (formerly Mother Huff's and later the Elms, see below) and the field now called Dr Joad's Hockey Pitch. It is not known if Erskine had the tunnel built but Repton advised him on his garden, which was called Evergreen Hill, presumably after the 'firs from Kew' which had been planted there but which no longer survive.

Compared to that of his friend and neighbour, Lord Mansfield, Erskine's property was modest, but it had splendid views each side of the 'Heights', to the north and also southwards, across the pastures of Kenwood in the foreground, with glimpses of the ponds and the great bank of South Wood in the middle ground and in the distance the new Fitzroy House on the slopes of Highgate.

Although a very successful advocate noted for his silver tongue,

The entrance to LORD CHANCELLOR ERSKINE'S Garden at Hampstead.

The view through the tunnel which connected Lord Erskine's House to his garden, Evergreen Hill, from the drawing by Repton.

Erskine was financially inept and by 1818 he was in difficulties. Lord Mansfield bought some if not all of Erskine's land in about 1820. For a while the house was occupied by Sir Nicholas Tindal, Chief Justice of the Common Pleas, who then built a house on the east side of the Spaniards Road, north of the Elms, hence 'Mount Tyndal' the modern apartment block on the site, though spelling seems not to have been the developer's strong point.

Continue to walk through the woodland, passing the apartment block of Mount Tyndal on your right, then the Elms.

On your right is the Elms itself, a Victorian house built on the site of Mother Huff's (see p.85), and named after a group of nine elms long since disappeared. The house and garden were extended several times and you can see part of the garden terracing. Between 1894 and 1908 Lord Duveen, art dealer and collector, lived here as a tenant of Lord Mansfield. It was he who advised Lord Iveagh on acquisitions to his collection, now hanging in Kenwood House.

As you reach the flatter ground you will become aware of a

change in the vegatation: conifers, laurel, yew and grey poplar tell you that you are in what was once a Victorian and then Edwardian garden, and now a gloomy and unwelcoming place.

When you reach this part of the Elms garden, turn sharp left and make your way back to the main path through West Meadow. Turn right onto the path and follow it to the Hampstead Gate into South Wood. Do not enter South Wood but follow the path through South Meadow, with South Wood on your left.

On your left you will be able to catch glimpses of the old wood bank (see page 45).

South Meadow can barely be described as meadow now but it was one, from the felling of the woodland in about 1600 until the 1960s, by which time the fields were no longer grazed or cut for hay. Regenerating woodland has now given it the character of wood pasture. When it was farmland it was divided into three fields, and a number of old hedgerow oaks can still be seen (see p.98). The field on the west part, which was divided into two, was known as Diana Field, after either the wife or daughter (both of whom were named Diana) of John Bill, son of the John Bill who built the first Kenwood House in the early seventeenth century. When it came to names they seem to have been a highly repetitive lot.

Soon after 1910 the meadow was a golf course, laid out by the Grand Duke Michael Romanov, cousin of Tsar Nicholas and exiled in England on account of an unsuitable marriage. He had become a tenant at Kenwood in 1910. He shared a passion for golf with his friend Arthur Crosfield, to whom we are indebted for saving the Kenwood estate for our enjoyment (see p.145). Grand Duke Michael was 6' 6" tall and had specially lengthened clubs.

When you reach the end of South Meadow, turn right onto the main path leading from South Wood back towards Parliament Hill, turning left onto the Boundary Path to reach the Boating Pond and the starting point at the entrance to Fitzroy Park.

Houses and Gardens of the Northern Heights: Golders Hill to Jack Straw's

2 km / 1 hour

This walk explores Golders Hill, the Pergola Garden of The Hill, the lost villas on the road to Jack Straw's Castle and returns via North End. It also reveals how the struggle to stamp out slavery was closely connected with this small area.

Start at the main entrance to Golders Hill Park on North End Road. As you go through the gate take the left fork (through the car park) and as the open lawn comes into view walk onto the grassy bank on your right staying on the high ground.

This is where a large and imposing Victorian mansion stood, looking down over a landscaped park, over tree tops to the distant countryside to the north and west. Without the house, the park lacks focus and no longer feels like a coherently designed landscape. But standing here and imagining the Victorian scene makes it easier to understand the park.

Golders Hill House, originally an eighteenth century dwelling, was bought in 1869 by Sir Thomas Spencer Wells, Surgeon to the Queen's Household. The house was altered and enlarged, and the gardens remodelled by the garden designer Robert Marnock, a

Golders Hill House, c1900.

leading proponent of a return to more naturalistic designs in contrast with the high Victorian fashion for elaborate bedding schemes in geometric patterns. In the 1870s another gardening expert, William Robinson, described the garden in glowing terms:

> 'As regards design and views it is the best garden with which I am acquainted in or near this sooty Babylon... An open lawn there is which rolls up to the house like a carpet, groups of fine trees, and wide and distant views.'

Until the end of the nineteenth century there were open views onto West Heath, and visitors remarked on the striking contrast between the rough gorse and heath clad common and the lush sylvan beauty of Golders Hill. The views are more restricted now but a tradition for planting unusual tree species has continued. As you walk around the park look out for the Dawyck Beech and the Cypress Oak near where the house stood, and the Turner's Oak near the lily pond.

When Spencer Wells died in 1897 the house and park were put up for auction. At this time property as close as this to London was being snapped up by developers, but Golders Hill was saved by the timely intervention of Thomas Barratt who bid for it on his own account when the bidding rose above the fund collected by local residents. Barratt, soap magnate and Hampstead historian was Chairman of A. & F. Pears. The famous soap advertisement, 'Bubbles' was based on a Millais portrait of Barratt's grandson. In 1899 the house and park were made over to the LCC for public enjoyment. In 1941 the house was destroyed by a parachute mine, and the park lost most of its coherence.

Walk briefly down the centre of the lawn and then join the path to your right which will take you down the hill and on anti-clockwise around the park. As you walk down the centre of the lawn watch out for the old thorn tree, marking the still visible line of the ha-ha that once divided the house and grounds from the deer park beyond.

The park had been laid out and the first Golders Hill House built in the 1760s on fields and manorial waste ground along the main route to Hendon, by Charles Dingley, a man who 'had a highly successful career as a slightly shady merchant and financier'. He had made a fortune out of trade with Russia, and had designed and built a windpowered sawmill at Limehouse. The rest of his story lies towards the end of the walk, in North End.

In the 1790s Humphry Repton was in vogue on the Northern Heights. As well as Fitzroy Park, Kenwood and Evergreen Hill, Repton worked at Golders Hill where his client, a Mr John Coore, '... retreated from business to enjoy the happiness of the society of his blooming wife and the possession of a blooming garden,' as Repton's memoir put it. There was no Red Book or other clues as to what he advised but by the early nineteenth century the park had matured into a picturesque landscape of lawn and meadows, and

Golders Hill House, Middx. The seat of John Coore, Esq. (W.Birch, c.1790)

ponds and groups of splendid trees, and walks which took you to all parts of the grounds and to the occasional summer house to rest and enjoy the unfolding scene.

Continue to walk down the hill. On your right you will pass the lily pond, the old walled garden and orchard.

In the early nineteenth century there was an extensive kitchen garden with hot houses, three vineries, a peach house, a mushroom house and potting sheds. Today the walled garden is a flower garden with a startling array of colours.

Keep following the path in the same direction passing the animal pens, a good way off at first, and eventually tennis courts on your right. Either go through the gate slightly on

your left and through the middle of the Water Garden, or if it is locked keep to the main path and pass the Water Garden on your left.

There was a small Victorian summer house on either side of this little valley which was wilder and more wooded with a string of three ponds.

Take the woodchip footpath immediately to your left as you leave the Water Garden on the far side of the valley. This path winds through the dell, crossing the stream which issues from the Leg O'Mutton Pond, and passes a graceful cut-leafed alder (just before turning left up the hill). Ignore the first exit from Golders Hill and keeping to the extreme right of the park, walk between the large holly bushes facing you, and along the narrow path between the deer enclosure on your left and the old boundary bank (and park perimeter) on your right. Leave Golders Hill Park through the gate on your right (there is a utility area just outside the gate). Cross Sandy Road and follow the winding footpath which leads you through the woods and up a gentle slope. When you see the wall of the Hill Garden, bear right and follow the wall round, turning left up a steep path until you come to the entrance to the Pergola on your left.

Part of the pleasure of this Italianate pergola is coming across it so unexpectedly. For many years this section was the only accessible part of this garden. The rest was boarded up – a mysterious and tangled ruin. Many of the columns which were straining under the weight of climbing plants finally collapsed in the 1987 storm. Elsewhere timbers had rotted and the terrace retaining walls were beginning to slip and crumble. A huge restoration programme was started in 1992 by the Corporation of London, and the Pergola

Garden was re-opened in 1995.

You are presently standing in the second stretch of the Pergola to be built. Although scheduled for eventual restoration, it is more mellow and therefore the best section to see first. Some of the climbers twining around the columns are the original plants.

Enter the Pergola, turn left and walk down to the Belvedere at the very end. Pause here and look out at Harrow-on-the-Hill.

This garden with its 800 foot pergola was designed by Thomas Mawson and constructed between 1905 and 1925. Mawson, known as 'the landscape architect of the Empire', had offices in Lancaster, London, Vancouver and Athens. The garden was part of The Hill, originally an eighteenth century house which was rebuilt in the 1890s and then transformed and extended by its new owner, another soap magnate, William Lever, later Lord Leverhulme, in 1905. Lever was a larger than life character with a huge appetite for building, garden making and garden parties.

The Hill was one of three gardens that Mawson designed for Leverhulme. Here at The Hill, he turned to gardens of the Italian Renaissance with their terraces, colonnades and pergolas for his inspiration. His designs were conceived as ways of extending the house into the landscape. The architectural elements provided a transition and structures for planting and acted as counterparts to the forms of nature. Some elements have an 'Arts and Crafts' feel about them, but Mawson was perhaps less successful at this than his contemporaries, Edwin Lutyens and Gertrude Jekyll. While Lutyens made the architectural design, Jekyll was the undisputed doyenne of planting layout in her day. Mawson mentions Jekyll once in his autobiography. 'There was a Miss Jekyll writing about daffodils ...' he wrote in what must rate as one of the classic put-downs.

The problem at The Hill was to create a garden where the parties and fetes could be held and where there was privacy without sacrificing the panoramic views over West Heath to Harrow and Windsor beyond. Mawson's solution was to build this raised terrace and pergola walk. By happy coincidence, just at the time that the garden was being planned, a 17 mile long tunnel was being dug for the extension of the Northern Line to Golders Green, and a huge quantity of spoil to raise the terrace was available to them without cost.

As you stand in the Belvedere facing Harrow, the garden on your right was the garden of Heath Lodge which once stood more or less where the rectangular pond is now. Heath Lodge was built in 1776 for a celebrity of the day, the actress Mrs Lessingham, through the influence of her lover Sir William Addington, a playwright and chief magistrate at Bow Street. Addington somehow acquired the large grant of two acres of the Heath from the lord of the manor though plots were usually only granted to existing copyholders. However, the building of the house did not proceed smoothly. Some copyholders took matters into their own hands. As the house was constructed by day, so it was pulled down by night. The matter at length came to court with victory for Mrs Lessingham and the house was duly completed (see map on p.129). Leverhulme acquired Heath Lodge in 1911, seven years after The Hill. He demolished it so as to extend his garden and the great pergola.

After enjoying the view from the Belvedere with the spire of Harrow in the distance, walk back along the Pergola, up the steps, and into the domed temple. Pause here to look beyond the bridge in front of you, to the wooden 'tented roofed temple'.

Once Leverhulme had bought Heath Lodge, Mawson had the challenge of linking it with, and incorporating it into, the existing garden of The Hill. One problem was the right of way (over which the bridge now passes) which the LCC had stubbornly refused to relinquish. A large conservatory stood on the site of the present tented roof temple, on the axis of the house and lily pond. Mawson decided to demolish it, replacing it with the tented roofed temple linked to the bridge and domed temple.

The other problem was one of orientation. As you stand in the domed temple you will see that the temple acts as a 'knuckle' at which the visual axis turns to line up with the Belvedere viewing terrace and Harrow-on-the-Hill. Continue over the bridge. From the tented temple turn right and continue walking along the Pergola until it turns again.

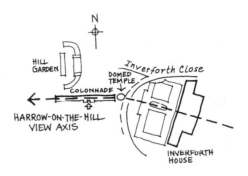

This was the extent of the first stage of garden construction. As you walk along the Pergola you can imagine the garden parties and fetes which became a regular feature of life at The Hill. The effect is rather inhibited by the steel treillage separating the pergola from the house beyond, now known as Inverforth House (after its last private owner, Lord Inverforth) which subsequently became a convalescent home and has now been converted into residences.

Continue southwards on the Pergola Walk through the Summer Pavilion and to the Belvedere at the end.

The adjacent property of Cedar Lawn was added to the garden in 1911, but work on this final stage of the Pergola was postponed until after the war and completed in 1925. Leverhulme died the following year. Sadly, Mawson used reconstituted stone for the columns and balustrades, not the creamy Whitbed Portland stone he had used for the first two stages. The Summer Pavilion was designed to look out over Cedar Lawn, but has now had its orientation reversed to look out over the trees of West Heath.

Descend by the spiral staircase. You may care to explore the garden below the Pergola, which has been re-designed in the style of the period.

This area, tucked out of sight of the main garden, was where the kitchen gardens were, along with potting sheds, greenhouses, a vinery, a mushroom house and all the clutter that went with a grand Edwardian garden. During restoration the whole of this undercroft was filled in with a lean mix concrete to stabilise the retaining walls.

Return to the bottom of the spiral staircase and leave the Pergola Garden by the iron gate. Turn left and walk up the slope to North End Way. Turn right and head for Jack Straw's Castle.

On your right you can see the only place around the perimeter of the Heath where the tide of bricks and mortar has receded. Here, from the late seventeenth century a hamlet of humble cottages became established probably as a result of a few squatters taking advantage of manorial disorganisation to encroach upon the waste. In the early eighteenth century it was the site of the ancient animal pound and poor houses and became known as Littleworth, presumably a commentary on the value placed upon this windswept piece of heath

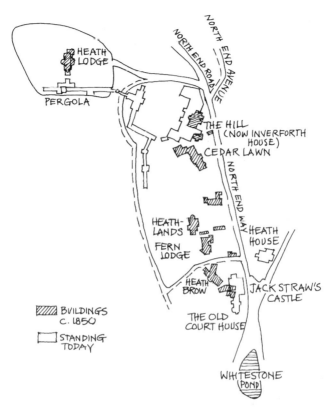

at the time. However, as Hampstead flourished the gentry moved in, and the cottages were upgraded to villas. If, in your sense of fair play, you are concerned that somehow the lord of the manor was woefully cheated by a surreptitious process, allay your fears. He did very nicely out of the rents he could obtain from these gentry encroachments onto what was, to him, largely unproductive land. By 1762 there were eleven houses between Jack Straw's and The Hill, and by the early nineteenth century Littleworth had become 'Heath Brow', the very name an indication of its gentrification.

Leverhulme had acquired and demolished Cedar Lawn, the

largest house next to The Hill in the 1920s. If you turn off the main road to your right, and explore the wooded slope you will find interesting remnants of Heathlands garden, a large 'cucumber' magnolia and a tulip tree hidden among the oaks and hollies of the regenerating woodland. The cucumber tree was introduced to Britain in 1736 and remains uncommon, but when it fruits it is well worth seeing, for these change from shocking pink to deep red, erect 'cucumbers'. Heathlands was home to a founder member of the Far East merchants, Jardine Matheson. Heathlands and the next house along, Fern Lodge, which had been built by Samuel Sotheby, the auctioneer, were destroyed by a parachute mine in 1941, and the land subsequently returned to the Heath. Jack Straw's and Heath House were also severely damaged, but the other house that was destroyed in the blast was Heath Brow, tucked behind Jack Straw's. The Heath Brow site is now a car park.

On reaching Jack Straw's, cross North End Way at the pedestrian crossing and stand in front of Heath House.

This 'large, square, somewhat grim-looking Georgian house', to quote Thomas Barratt, saviour of Golders Hill, was the home of the Quaker banker and philanthropist, Samuel Hoare. Hoare had moved from Stoke Newington to enjoy the fresh air and views of Heath House from which, it was boasted, one could see no fewer than six counties. Hoare was frequent host to local literary luminaries but, more significantly, to those who passionately deplored the slave trade, notably William Wilberforce and Thomas Clarkson, the two most eminent Abolitionists, and also local stalwarts such as Mrs Barbauld and the young Thomas Fowell Buxton, of whom more anon.

As you begin to make your way back along North End Way, on the Heath House side of the road, give another glance at the Heath Brow car park behind Jack Straw's.

At the end of the eighteenth century two villa cottages stood there, in one of which lived William Grenville, who headed the 'Ministry of All the Talents', 1806-7. Grenville had himself long deplored the slave trade, and almost certainly had joined Hoare's anti-slave trade gatherings. It was on the last day of his ministry that his bill proscribing the trade received the royal assent. Grenville resigned that day because he refused to be silent on the question of Catholic emancipation, as had been demanded of him by George III. In so doing, Grenville effectively destroyed his own political career. Hampstead's liberal tradition has worthy antecedents.

The road leading to North End. The two Gibbet Elms stand on the left of the road, while on the right may be seen fencing marking the beginning of North End Avenue. (G. Childs, c. 1840)

Make your way along the road. After the end of Heath House garden, note the open paddock which once belonged to The Hill, and was incorporated into the Heath straight after Leverhulme's death in 1925. Just as North End Way curves down into the cutting, take North End Avenue, the lime avenue forking off to your right.

North End Avenue was the main road until North End Way was — somewhat inexplicably — cut through the steepest part of the hill, in about 1730. This lane connected with Wyldes, and possibly from there the road ran across the present Heath Extension to Wild Hatch (see p. 162), or the old road may have gone more directly down the hill behind Manor House Hospital and King Alfred's School, which both front onto North End Road. A large wild service tree lurking behind the second lime on the left bank indicates that this lane is probably very old. North End itself only became a hamlet in the seventeenth century, and remained predominantly a village of agricultural labourers and laundresses until the mid-nineteenth century.

The lime avenue is worth seeing in late spring for the sheer intensity of green foliage. As you descend the limes give way to sweet and horse chestnuts. On your left are the surviving remnants of Pitt House garden. This is all that is left of Pitt House, the property which Charles Dingley at Golders Hill lent to Pitt the Elder, as a refuge during his breakdown in the mid-1760s. Dingley seems to have been anxious to ingratiate himself with Pitt with a view to becoming a member of Parliament. His career in politics, however, was shortlived, for he was fatally injured in an affray at the hustings in Brentford in 1769, while opposing the formidable John Wilkes as parliamentary candidate for Middlesex. Pitt House itself was demolished in 1952.

As you approach the crossroads at the bottom of the avenue, note the last house on your right, now called Cedar Lodge, but previously Byron Cottage.

This was the home of yet another high-minded Quaker reformer, Thomas Fowell Buxton. With a sister-in-law called Elizabeth Fry, it is no surprise that Buxton made his name as a prison reformer. However, in 1824 he took over leadership of the Commons anti-slavery party, at Wilberforce's request, and saw his task to a successful conclusion with the abolition of slavery in 1833. Thus the Northern Heights proved not only a country retreat for the magnate class but also the scene for the most decisive advances in human rights in that epoch.

Return along North End to North End Road.

WALK 9 *The Heath saved*

4.5 km / 1.75 hrs

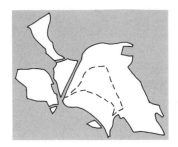

This walk covers the broad outline of how the Heath became public property, but omits 'pocket handkerchief' plots added over the past century or so.

BEFORE YOU WALK

Hampstead had become highly fashionable as a spa in the early eighteenth century but essentially for pleasurable forays out of London. By the beginning of the nineteenth century, however, Hampstead was rapidly acquiring a resident population of City grandees and other gentry who preferred to live in Hampstead than in the pollution and filth of the City. Some of these gentry were tenants, or 'copyholders', of the Lord of the Manor, Sir Thomas Maryon Wilson, others were simply Hampstead residents. Like all his predecessors, Sir Thomas was an absentee, living in Kent.

By the 1820s London was expanding rapidly, and landlords in its purlieus were busily selling or leasing their lands (both demesne and common lands) to developers. In this respect Sir Thomas was no different from his contemporaries. In three vital respects, however, he found himself critically impeded in his intention of realising the value of his estate. First, the trust clauses in his father's will prevented him from both leasing land for more than 21 years, and from selling any part of the estate. His second impediment was that he lacked the capital to develop the estate himself. His third problem was that unlike many other landlords on the fringes of London he had articulate and influential residents to deal with.

With the Finchley Road now being cut across the farmland below Hampstead, Sir Thomas presented a Private Bill to Parliament in 1829 listing the land he wished to develop. Tacked to the bottom of the list were the words 'The Heath and other waste land or ground in the Manor, whether occupied or not.' It was this fatal clause which led Hampstead residents, including his more influential tenants, to get the Bill thrown out of the Commons. He was also opposed by the 3rd Earl Mansfield at Kenwood, who knew Maryon Wilson was attempting to breach the terms of his father's will, and had no wish to have his own estate hemmed in with unsightly modern housing. 'I oppose you on private grounds,' he declared, 'but I will put it on public ground, and I know I can beat you.' And he was right. Sir Thomas made repeated attempts the following year and also in 1843 and 1844. Under the 1236 Statute of Merton, his ownership of the common (i.e. West and Sandy Heaths and part of East Heath) and his right to exploit it was a principle which he was unwilling to concede. His obstinacy proved his undoing, and the contest became bitter.

Start on the Spaniards Road opposite the east flank of Heath House (near the Whitestone Pond). Start walking down the Viaduct Road towards the Viaduct.

Sir Thomas was incensed by the opposition he encountered from the Heath-loving gentry and he decided to exploit it himself. First he arranged for the excavation of larger quantities of sand than ever before from Sandy Heath. And he decided to change the character of the Heath by planting exotic trees, of which the fir trees on the escarpment are one example, the line of Lucombe oaks on the far side of the Upper Fairground probably another, as well as a large number of Turkey oaks, robinias and also many willows along the Hampstead brook.

Pause as you pass the Upper Fairground and look out for a brick 'pepperpot' hut below the track on your right, and a ha-ha, buttressed by a brick wall half-hidden in the undergrowth, running from the hut down to the embankment of the Vale of Health Pond.

It will be recalled from the map on page 79, that this is where the heath or common ends, and part of the lord's demesne land begins. In 1844 Sir Thomas decided to begin developing on his demesne land out of his own pocket. He planned an estate of 28 villas, and christened it East Park. The hut and ha-ha probably mark the beginning of the intended development, which he commenced without informing anyone. The plan (opposite) shows a drive (now the Viaduct Road) running through the middle of an estate which would probably have rivalled Bishops Avenue in sumptuous magnificence. Each villa would have stood in two acres of grounds.

As you continue, note opposite the Ladies' lavatory a large robinia (false acacia), possibly from the original planting. The public toilets are worth a quick glance, a nice example of late Victorian/early Edwardian mock Tudor outside, original tiles and gas lamps inside. The enclosure in which the toilets are situated was originally established by Maryon Wilson as a plant nursery for the intended estate.

Walk down to the Viaduct.

The most ambitious part of the project was to carry a road across the swampy ground draining into the valley. The ground was drained to

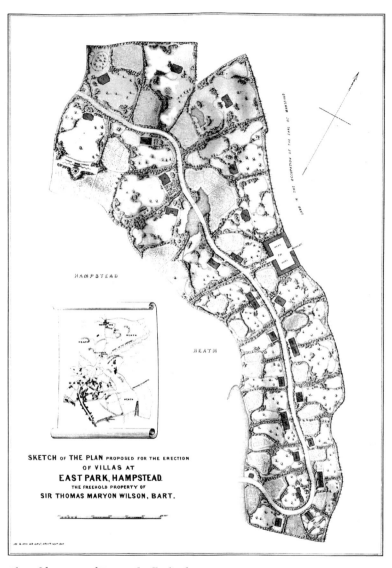

Plan of the proposed East Park villa development.

form an ornamental pond, and the viaduct built from bricks dug and fired on site. (The sandstone pillars at either end are from the Midlands coal measures.) However, the project did not go well: the foundation excavations collapsed repeatedly and it was three years before the viaduct was finally built. 'Wilson's Folly', as it was then known, exhausted Sir Thomas' resources and in 1853 he made yet another fruitless attempt to get a Bill through Parliament. This time the opposition was led by the banker John Gurney Hoare, who lived at The Hill (the site is now occupied by Inverforth House), and was son of Samuel Hoare (see p.130). Once again it was thrown out, after a press campaign against it. By now defence of the Heath had become a *cause célèbre*. Sir Thomas rashly refused offers of compromise that would have allowed him to develop other areas of his estate, and his subsequent attempts to worst his opponents over the next decade were similarly frustrated.

Thoroughly thwarted, Sir Thomas now resorted to despoliation. In 1866 the Midland Railway required enormous quantities of sand and gravel to extend its line to the new terminus of St Pancras. Sir Thomas obliged, with 30 cartloads of sand being removed daily from Sandy Heath (see p.17), severely damaging the tree, gorse and heather cover.

Continue down the Viaduct Road to the Football Field. As you approach the crossing with the Boundary Path, note a magnificent plane tree on your left, possibly another of Maryon Wilson's exotic plantings.

Sir Thomas' other great despoliation in the mid-1860s was to grant a 21 year lease (the maximum allowable under his father's will) on the lands of East Park below the Viaduct to a local builder for use as brickfields. It is the consequent excavation that accounts for the Football Field cut from the hillside and the broken ground below the

The brickfield on East Park, c. 1880. Rows of bricks are drying before firing.

Viaduct Road down to the Hampstead brook gully.

Geologically, the site was ideal for brickmaking, since it is a Claygate Bed, a mixture of sand and clay. (Unadulterated London Clay is unsuitable. It is naturally blue, being rich in iron sulphide which turns a familiar ochre as it becomes sulphate on exposure to the air. The inherent sulphate would cause the bricks to burst on firing.) The clay was dug out on site, the sulphates flushed out by rainfall, and then mixed with surface silt from the Claygate Bed, and with chalk and ash. The silt and chalk reduced the tendency to crack during drying and to burst during firing. The ash contained fine coal dust which helped achieve a high temperature within the bricks, and left cinder marks in the finished product. The bricks were fired in open 'clamps', piles of up to 100,000 dried bricks with layers of cinders between the courses. Several flues would be left open and filled with brushwood. Once the clamp was well alight, the flues were closed and the clamp allowed to burnt itself out over the next four weeks. The chalk, turning to silicate lime, ensured the familiar yellow of London stocks, but the colour was also affected by temperature and the amount of air to which the bricks are exposed during firing. Such clamps produced a terrible stench. Many of the bricks closest to the burning brushwood overheated and warped and were sold off cheaply for garden rockeries. Spoilt bricks may still be seen built into the Boundary Path and other paths on the old brickyard site just below the Viaduct Pond.

There were dozens of similar brickfields around the fringes of London at the time, producing 500 million bricks yearly by the 1860s. Teams of men, women and children worked from 4.30am until 8.00pm. As one foreman told inspectors, 'One half-hour at 3pm is the only real meal time they have in the day.' They were paid per thousand bricks, a team of six producing 3,500 unfired bricks a day, or up to one million a year, in their wooden moulds, or 'stocks'. Beer shops used to set up on site, which became notorious for drunken behaviour. It is difficult now to associate the Heath with such human exploitation and degradation.

Proceed along the Viaduct Road into the cutting.

During the period of brickmaking, a rail track was apparently laid to transport the bricks down to South End, presumably to Hampstead Heath station.

Follow the track down to the causeway between the Mixed Bathing Pond and Pond No 2. Pause on the causeway.

The threat posed to the Heath was also faced by many of the old commons surrounding London. Many were developed before they could be protected, but in 1865 the Commons Preservation Society was formed to assist local groups protect their commons from enclosure and development. Hampstead Heath was at the forefront of the battle. In 1866 Sir Thomas started building by the Flagstaff at the Whitestone Pond, invoking his rights as Lord of the Manor and it was decided to challenge him in the Courts, but his death three years later spared the campaigners a long and costly struggle. His successor, his brother Sir John, sold the manorial rights over the 220 acres of Hampstead common land to the Metropolitan Board of Works. The Hampstead Heath Act of 1871 stipulated that 'the Board shall at all times preserve, as far as may be, the natural aspect and state of the Heath, and to that end shall protect the turf, heather, timber and other trees, shrubs and brushwood thereon.' Thus all the heathland, Sandy, West and part of East Heath including the ponds, all of which had been dug mainly out of the common, became public property.

Retrace your steps but after 100 metres fork right and walk to the corner of the back gardens of South Hill Park Gardens, at the foot of Parliament Hill.

In 1886 the lease on the East Park brickfield was due to expire, with a real danger that East Park would finally be developed. Moreover, it was feared that the 4th Earl Mansfield might sell Parliament Hill Fields for development. He had already allowed the development of the bottom of these fields as far as his boundary, Mansfield Road, for housing and for the railway.

It was now that three great figures in conservation, George Shaw-Lefevre and Robert Hunter of the Commons Protection Society, and Octavia Hill, the housing reformer (the latter two being co-founders of the National Trust), decided on a strategy to save these lands from development. It was crucial to obtain both estates together, since the purchase of only one would greatly enhance the development value of the other.

In fact Sir Spencer Maryon Wilson, Sir John's successor, now had limited options. The loss of the Heath meant that access to East Park was eliminated on the west and most of the north side, except for the narrow neck of land close to the Spaniards Inn. In 1871 access from the south was lost. For that year Thomas Rhodes, the owner of the fields immediately south of East Park, developed his plot into the bizarrely-shaped South Hill Park. This made development of East Park almost impossible, although Rhodes seems not to have realized this. (Had he done so, he would surely have faced his houses outwards onto open meadows instead of in their present enclosed manner.) Drainage was the crucial issue. Between 1859 and 1865 Joseph Bazalgette had laid the London sewer system we still use today. With piped water and flush lavatories, proper drains connecting into that system were essential. If drains could be cut into those laid for South Hill Park, it might still be possible to develop East Park. Yet road access could only be achieved through Lord Mansfield's estate. The road called Parliament Hill from South End and also Nassington Road clearly anticipated Lord Mansfield's development of Parliament Hill Fields. But he proved more interested in protecting the southern edge of the Kenwood estate, and could now do so profitably by selling the fields south of what we now call South Meadow (previously Diana Field, see p.118), not to developers but to conservationists.

Denied either drainage or road access, development of East Park ceased to be an option. Thus, a deal was struck both with Mansfield and Maryon Wilson, and in 1889 sufficient money was raised from local government and from individual gifts to purchase both estates, increasing the overall size of the Heath to 481 acres.

Turn up the tarmac path in the direction of South Wood. After about 250 metres as the path rises more steeply you will see the Tumulus with its fir trees. Make for it. (As you walk savour the subtle change in grass quality, as one ascends onto Bagshot Sand.)

The Tumulus remains the Heaths's best known mystery. What really was it? The idea that it was an iron age barrow probably originated with the antiquarian William Stukeley, who drew the mound in 1725, concluding 'It was the tumulus of some ancient British king before Christianity, probably enough, of Immanuence monarch here just before Caesar's invasion.' Imanuentis was leader of the Trinobantes, defending the London area against the Catuvellauni, whose main centre was near St Albans at the time of Caesar's invasion in 54 BC.

With the possibility that the Tumulus might become public property, wild surmise was renewed. William Howitt had already set the ball rolling in his book *The Northern Heights* (1869), with the theory that the people of St Albans sought to defeat their rivals the people of London here, but were defeated and 'this mound contains the dust of the slain.' In November 1883 John Hales, professor of English Literature at King's College London, added his own speculation, writing in *The Athenaeum* 'One ... may perhaps plausibly conjecture that it was the very battle in which fell King Imanuentius himself.' His febrile imagination envisaged the bellicose Catuvellauni 'making for London, when the Londoners, marching up the valley, met them at this spot and dyed the stream with their own and their enemies' blood.' Another persistent popular rumour was that Boudicea, Queen of the Iceni, was buried here. In 1894, the mound was excavated by Hercules Read, Keeper of British and medieval antiquities at the British Museum. Stukeley's mound by this time was substantially larger, and two feet below the surface

Read found a layer of black soil: 'In this blackened stratum were found stems and bowls of old tobacco pipes, of probably the beginning of the last century.' He also reported finding fragments of Chinese porcelain and Delft ware, but he found nothing to suggest anything older. It was with sublime disregard for this lack of evidence that Read (later Sir Hercules) concluded that the Tumulus was 'very probably an ancient British burial mound of the early bronze age.' Whatever lurks underneath, much of it seems to be an eighteenth century rubbish tip.

Another theory, that it is the foundation for a windmill is also unsatisfactory. Until the end of the sixteenth century the area probably remained woodland, so it would presumably have been built thereafter (unless the area had been cleared in the early fourteenth century only to be re-forested after the Black Death). It is barely credible that all memory of a windmill had been lost by Stukeley's time, unless the windmill had been very shortlived. But why have a windmill when the woodland was cut down only for pasture and meadow? In any case, there was little need for a windmill. Water mills on both tributaries of the Fleet were the obvious option (land drains since the nineteenth century have greatly reduced both streams). Perhaps it was never more than a romantic feature, possibly fashioned from detritus following the felling of the woodland. It is faintly possible it was a folly to be viewed from Kenwood House, for it seems there was once a cutting through South Wood which may have been cut once the wood became essentially ornamental in the early seventeenth century.

Pass the Tumulus on its east (Highgate) side and continue in the same (diagonal) direction across the field, across the Boundary Path and into the gully of South Meadow.

This gully, with its hedgerow line, marks the limit of what was incorporated into the Heath in 1889. Up to your left the new border with Mansfield's remaining estate swung up almost to South Wood's Hampstead Gate, curving across Diana Field in order to achieve a harmonious new boundary to this public space.

Continue across South Meadow, veering slightly right to reach the Highgate Gate of South Wood.

The story of the saving of the rest of the Mansfield estate is too long to tell here except in outline. The 6th Earl inherited Kenwood in 1906, but his life was centred on Scone Palace, the Murrays' Perthshire family seat. He rarely came south and had no attachment to Kenwood. He had been thinking about selling the estate in 1910, but the war had intervened and it was only afterwards that he sought to sell it, at an asking price of £550,000, the equivalent of about £22 million today. The threatened development would not only have destroyed the Kenwood estate, but by overlooking Parliament Hill Fields it would have destroyed the character of much of the Heath. Thus, the gains of the previous 50 years suddenly seemed in jeopardy.

Enter Arthur Crosfield, a rich, cultured and sensitive man from a Merseyside Quaker and soap manufacturing family.

Look eastwards across the valley to Highgate.

On the skyline stands Witanhurst (41 West Hill), Crosfield's 'monument to a disastrous love'. For he built it for his beautiful, talented but faithless wife, Domini, who demanded of him the largest private house in London. Witanhurst is our only visible reminder of the man who, with skill and patience, masterminded a campaign involving royalty, nobility and multi-millionaires.

In 1919, when the sale of Kenwood seemed imminent, Crosfield, with the help of Robert Waley-Cohen (of Caen Wood Towers, now Athlone House), Henry Goodison (Fitzroy Park) and an Australian, Lawrence Chubb (founder of the Ramblers Association and secretary to the National Trust), launched the Kenwood Preservation Council for a cause that many thought hopeless. There would be no government funds and the London County Council (LCC) showed little enthusiasm. Mansfield eventually agreed with Crosfield a lower price of £340,000 for a limited period. Appeals were launched, but only £53,000 had been raised by the time the option to buy had expired.

When all seemed lost, Crosfield adopted an entirely new strategy, to negotiate for parts of the estate on a piecemeal basis, and he turned to his northern industrialist friends for the money. With help from magnates in Harrogate, Liverpool, Carnforth and Paisley, Crosfield negotiated the purchase of South Meadow and all the eastern side of the estate, including Lord Southampton's former parkland, now known as Cohen's Fields, in 1922. At first glance this plot might seem the least important part of the whole estate. In fact Crosfield was a brilliant tactician, for without this land Mansfield would face major drainage problems in any housing development at Kenwood.

Enter South Wood by the Highgate Gate. Turn left immediately and walk 200 metres before taking the first turn to the right.

The Kenwood Preservation Council was now able to persuade Mansfield to agree to a covenant for the permanent preservation of a strip of South Wood running along its southern edge in return for its support for the consent which he desired from the LCC to lay a drain across the Heath to connect to the Vale of Health sewer. The covenant was crucial for protecting the skyline of the Heath as already gained. The projected drain was crucial to Mansfield's residual development plan.

Turn left at the T-junction 200 metres on, and walk down to the Stone Bridge.

The South Wood preservation covenant drastically reduced South Wood's building value. Moreover, in offering support for Mansfield's application for a drain, the Council almost certainly knew that the LCC was most unlikely to approve the application. To that extent the Council was guilty of duplicity, albeit in the public interest. By the time Mansfield learnt that he had been outmanoeuvred, his Hampstead factor had already drawn up a development plan for 33 villas on North Wood and West Meadow. With South Wood no longer feasible for development, Mansfield agreed to sell the rest of it to the Kenwood Preservation Council, the ponds and a strip of the Pasture Ground north of it, in 1924.

Turn left from the Pasture Ground into West Meadow at the first opportunity and cross it to West Field Gate. Turn right and follow the path across the Upper Fairground site and to the starting point at the top of the Viaduct Road.

The Council handed over its acquisitions to the LCC and disbanded itself, safe in the still secret knowledge that the Earl of Iveagh had also negotiated with Mansfield for the remaining grounds and, above all, the House in order to house his collection of pictures as a bequest to the nation. Thus the residue of the estate was also saved for the public in early 1925.

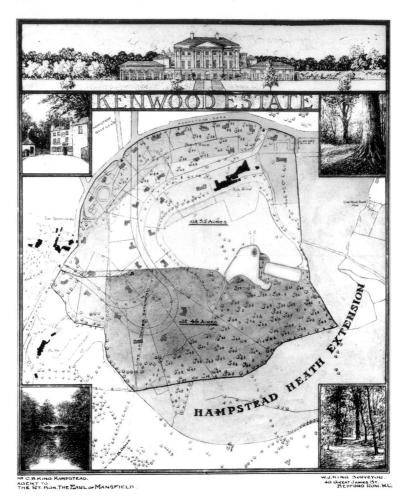

Plan of the proposed Kenwood villa development, c. 1923.

Waley Cohen is commemorated in Cohen's Fields. At the foot of those fields stands the Goodison fountain, commemorating Henry Goodison, Treasurer of the Kenwood Preservation Council. Yet today Crosfield, who did more than anyone, is barely remembered. The last years of this exceptional man were beset by depression and financial disaster. He died falling or jumping from the midnight Geneva express to Cannes in 1938.

10

The Heath Extension

2.5 km / 1.75 hours

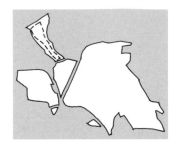

BEFORE YOU WALK

Except for those who live close to it, the Heath Extension has always been a poor relation to the rest of the Heath, yet it certainly has its own delights.

The Extension was saved thanks largely to the future doyenne of the Garden Suburb, Henrietta Barnett, a woman of great energy, remembered by a neighbour as 'a benevolent tyrant – a domineering woman – the equal of Queen Mary [George v's consort] – one who always believed she was right – a woman who would have her own way – a fascinating person because she was so outrageous – she did not care what she said where she was or who was present.' She was also, thankfully, a bit of a nimby. She and her husband, Samuel, a remarkable and saintly Anglican priest, spent most of the week in the working class parish of St Jude's, Whitechapel, but sought refreshment from their endeavours in their Hampstead retreat. This was Heath End House at the Spaniards which, with blithe understatement, they rechristened 'St Jude's Cottage'. For twenty or so years their energies were almost wholly absorbed in seeking to moderate the acute social deprivation of Whitechapel at that time. Samuel was a moving spirit behind the foundation of both Toynbee Hall and the Whitechapel Art Gallery.

Henrietta Barnett's first intimation that the magnificent view of farmland to the north of her weekend retreat might be in danger was from a chance conversation with a fellow traveller on board a ship bound for Russia in 1896. From him she heard that the Tube Railway Company had in mind the extension of the Charing Cross, Euston and Hampstead Railway northwards to North End and Golders Green, still open countryside at that time. At the time the company was still tunnelling towards Hampstead.

Rumour turned to fact when the proposed extension was sanctioned by Act of Parliament in 1902. It was learnt that a station was planned at North End, apparently with a vehicle park on the very ground where the 300-year old Wyldes farmhouse stood, and that negotiations were already under way with the owner of the Wyldes estate, Eton College.

Henrietta Barnett moved quickly, forming a Hampstead Heath Extension Council with the aim of purchasing the 80 acres of Wyldes farmland immediately adjacent to Sandy Heath. To give the proposed purchase greater political momentum she announced her plan for a model 'garden suburb for all classes' on the remaining 243 acres of the Eton estate. She realised that this would attract much more wholehearted support from the London County Council, and from the councillors of Hampstead and Hendon. As she informed the Provost of Eton, 'The Garden Suburb would benefit from the Heath Extension and that unless a definitive option to purchase those 243 acres for that purpose could be given to the Garden Suburb Trustees, both schemes would undoubtedly fall through.' It was with this double scheme in mind that Eton agreed to sell 80 acres for a 'heath extension' for only £36,000, with the proviso that the purchasers would also have to lay roads as specified around the west, south and east sides of the extension. The sum required was raised just before expiry of the agreed time limit and the property purchased and handed over to the LCC in 1907.

Golders Hill had already been saved for the public, in 1898. There could now no longer be housing for sufficient people to justify a tube station at North End, and plans for the 'Bull and Bush', as it was to be called, were abandoned. The platforms, however, had already been built and may be glimpsed en route in the tunnel as one rattles along the Northern Line.

Eton College had held Wyldes ever since 1449, initially as the appointed custodian for the estates of the Leper Hospital of St James, Westminster, a twelfth century foundation 'for fourteen Sisters, maidens that were leprous….living chastely and honestly in divine service'. This hospital had been located at a safe distance from London, but close to the Abbey of Westminster. St James's Hospital probably acquired Wyldes in the thirteenth century by which time, incidentally, the Sisters had blotted their copybook in the chastity department, having allowed certain Brothers into their houses.

In 1531 Eton was required to surrender St James' Leper Hospital and its adjacent fields to Henry VIII for a new royal estate, including the future St James' Palace. However, it was allowed to retain Wyldes and another of the hospital's holdings, Chalcotts (Chalk Farm). Wyldes was enlarged, probably in the late sixteenth century, by the addition of the farmland of Temple Fortune – an estate once assigned to the Knights Templar. From the seventeenth century onwards Eton rented parcels of Wyldes to tenants. This walk is intended to rediscover the farmland that lies beneath the present Extension, and for this reason the field names, mostly from the eighteenth century, are marked on the adjoining sketch map.

Start: This walk begins at the south east corner of the Heath Extension, at the sharp corner of Wildwood Road before it runs northwards.

It will be recalled from Walk No. 5 that the boundary between the ancient manors of Hendon and Hampstead (and the present boroughs of Camden and Barnet) runs along the bank between the south stretch of Wildwood Road and the Cooling Track.

Walk up to the end of the side-turning 'Wildwood Rise' and look through the gates of the sumptuous modern mansion beyond.

The line of the gates and fence marks the boundary between the manors of Hendon and Finchley. These met the Hampstead manor boundary about 50 metres along the wall to the right, known in Saxon times as Sandgate. Sandgate is an appropriate name. The Saxons were well aware that the soil quality changes around here, from sand (Claygate Beds) to London Clay (see Walk No.1) on the slope down to Mutton Brook, flowing beside Lyttleton Road/ Falloden Way/the North Circular and eventually into the river Brent.(Mutton Brook, incidentally, acquired its name through its use for sheep-dipping in the middle ages.)

The Saxon boundary was probably a hedgebank with a ditch. The two great oak trees just to your right may be part of the ancient Hendon-Finchley boundary bank. After this part of Finchley became the Bishop of London's deer park (see p.76) in the early middle ages, there would probably have been a deer-proof paling fence on the bank, set between two ditches. Deer farming was abandoned in the mid-fifteenth century.

On the left, beyond the skating pond, stand the oaks of Turner's Wood, named after the eighteenth century inhabitant of the Firs (see p. 37), but known at the time as Patrick Hill Wood and Hampstead Moors. It is almost certainly ancient woodland, and probably part of the more extensive woodland straddling the manorial boundary, probably loosely known as Wyldes Wood or Weild Wood (see below). However, a boundary ditch and bank would have run through the woodland between the two manors.

Retrace your steps down to Wildwood Road.

On the Hendon side of the boundary the whole area from Sandgate, westwards along the Hampstead manor boundary to Wyldes, and northwards along the Hendon-Finchley boundary as far as the hedgerow line bisecting the present Fairway Close was 'Wyldes Wood' (or Weild Wood) proper. Its western boundary ran up the track from the present Changing Rooms back to Wyldes. Wyldes Wood, about 34 acres in size, was felled in the 1550s by John Slannyng, the tenant at the time. It will be recalled from Walk No.6 that Slannyng got into trouble in 1556 for felling 20 acres of Kenwood. Slannyng had also cut down 'xiiii acres of wood in a wood called Wyldes Wood two yeres past' and 'he hath felled and cut down this yere xx acres', 34 acres in all. Although against the law, it had become more profitable to use the land as cattle pasture. Besides felling the coppice (see p. 38) he 'doithe put in his catell this last wynter soo that the sprynges [coppice stool shoots] are sore eaten in the same wood' and 'hath left no standers [grown timber trees] but young saplings in Wyldes Wood.' Slannyng left behind the 'ghosts' of the old woodland in the form of hedgerow lines.

Cross over and walk 50 metres down to the hedgerow and stream. Cross the stream and begin to follow its west bank downstream.

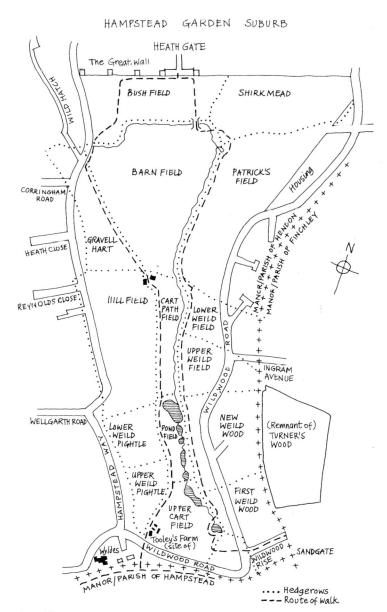

The field pattern and names predating the Extension.

This stream and the pond are evidence of the soil change, with water springing out of the ground as it hits the first strata of clay, near the foot of the Claygate Bed level.

Go around the west side of the first pond, and cross its 'weir' to the east bank.

There are very few ponds anywhere which are natural. Almost all are man-made [see p.20], in order to drain surrounding boggy ground, to provide a drinking reservoir for livestock, or a habitat for ducks. This first pond is the only one of the 'Seven Sisters', as these ponds are known, which is at least 250 years old. The rest were dug in 1908-9 by unemployed labourers.

Continue parallel to the stream bed. Move up to the path on your right as the stream becomes more difficult to follow (although you will continue to follow the stream line across the Extension). Stick to the main path, and resist the temptation to slip down to your left along the very edge of the second pond. As you begin to pass this second pond a few yards away on your left you should be walking along a path edged on its left by an old bank with oaks on it. It is in fact an old hedgerow line.

Note a very substantial bank running off to the right, up to Wildwood Road. It has an old coppiced hazel on the bank and at the end the huge dead stump of an old oak. This hedgerow bank divided two of the several fields probably created by Slannyng's felling of Wyldes Wood, their origin commemorated in the field names that continued to be used. This bank in fact divides First Weild Wood from New Weild Wood. All this side of the extension may have been under the plough by the eighteenth century as a contemporary map suggests, but it is extremely difficult now to tell.

Continue along the path running parallel to the ponds, with a hedgerow bank still on your left. (The path is joined by the horse track.)

Admire some of the fine old oak trees (both sessile and pedunculate; for the difference see p.43) on the hedgerow bank as you walk. If you are interested in the wild service tree (see p.46), watch out for the gap between ponds Nos. 5 and 6 (and if necessary retrace your steps to count the ponds carefully). Here in the old hedgerow bank, stands a pair of fine mature examples, with their distinctive bark, an indicator that this hedgerow bank is ancient, and may well be a ghost of ancient woodland.

Continue following the horse track parallel to the stream line. As you emerge from woodland on your right, you pass the old hedgerow line between New Weild Wood and Upper Weild Field, and a couple of paces further on your left, the hedgerow line between Pond Field and Cart Path Field.

Note after another 100 metres or so, a stream and another hedgerow running in obliquely from Ingram Avenue. It will be recalled that the manor and parish boundary between Hendon and Finchley ran along the back gardens of the houses fronting onto Wildwood Road, and all comprised Eton College's property of Wyldes. Why did it not all become Heath Extension?

From the sketch map it will be seen that the fields of Wyldes extended both west and east of the present Extension. Originally Henrietta Barnett had intended the purchase of 80 acres running down from the Hampstead boundary across the whole width of Wyldes, as far as, or a bit beyond the present Changing Rooms.

The decision to change the configuration was essentially financial. She and her council had proved unable to raise sufficient money for the total Wyldes frontage. The financial virtue of laying out finely designed housing along the frontage of the Extension was that it would greatly enhance the value of this surrounding land. This became integral to the whole Garden Suburb concept. Eton College could offset the relatively cheap price of the Extension itself, by the added value of the future mansions, houses and apartments that would overlook the Extension. On the 1905 plan, Henrietta Barnett scrawled across the area between Wildwood Road and Finchley parish boundary the words: 'This is the high ridge from whence some of the most distant views are obtained – and on which the rich will build their homes.' In fact the narrower but longer parcel of open land proved an aesthetic improvement.

Continue walking along the horsetrack parallel to the stream line. After approximately 100 metres pause by the next hedgerow line coming in from the right.

This is another old field hedge with three surviving oak trees. But it is the aspens, with leaves that shimmer and rustle more than any other member of the poplar family, which are of most interest. The only other group of aspens on the Heath are just to the west of the Vale of Health pond. Aspens were an early 'pioneer' species, arriving in Britain about 10,000 years ago when it was still joined to the continent. They spread by sucker and by seed and are often found in colonies in ancient woodland and in open heathy woodland where there is a wet clay subsoil. They are essentially northern trees and are relatively rare in south-east England. We know aspens grew in the area in Saxon times, for the Bleccanham boundary ran from Sandgate to 'a crooked aspen' (roughly where Kingsley Way and Wildwood Road meet).

Leave the horse track as it turns left, turning right into Patrick's Field. Continue to follow the stream line, remaining on the east side of the stream and hedgerow, much of which is composed of elm suckers.

The suckers are all that is left of a fine line of hedgerow elms, victims of Dutch elm disease. The elms were sufficiently tall that they had to be lopped during the Second World War so as not to inhibit the easterly angle of fire for the anti-aircraft guns sited on the Extension (see below).

Now a sports field, the barely perceptible ripples on the ground, running west-east, might possibly be traces of ploughing in the early eighteenth century. Its old name may be by association, for Bunker Hill was once known as Patrick's Hill. At the end of the hedgeline is a small pond at least 250 years old, but re-dug in 1996.

Continue past the pond, then turn left to follow the path alongside the hedgerow running westwards towards Hampstead Way. After 100 metres turn right across the footbridge and walk alongside the hedgerow line up to 'The Great Wall'.

You will note that while to the left the wall extends to Hampstead Way, to the right there are only hedges and gates. The Great Wall was intended to be one of the outstanding architectural features of the Suburb. Raymond Unwin, who designed the overall layout for the Suburb, very much wanted to make a statement of the conjunction between Suburb and Heath Extension. His inspiration came from medieval Bavarian hilltop towns. 'Though we shall not copy the fortified wall of the old city,' he wrote, '... the retaining wall may be a charming boundary, its monotony broken by garden houses and gates instead of turrets and bastions.' This is the effect

Unwin's Great Wall, as illustrated by his assistant, Charles Wade. Unwin wrote: 'In old towns which we admire ... we notice that the country comes up clean and fresh right to the point where the town proper begins ... In the oldest cities we sometimes find a wall with the country coming right up to the gates, which adds to the effect.' The spire of St Jude's as originally conceived differs from Edwin Lutyens' final version.

he sought here, with the high brick wall studded with gazebos and pavilions. But only a third was completed before World War dismissed the completion of such aesthetic trifles. Thus the east end remains unfinished and comparatively understated.

Turn left and begin walking alongside the Great Wall.

Most importantly, however, Unwin did achieve the shallow-stepped central gateway with its vista up to St Jude's. (It was intended to achieve vistas for Linnell, Turner and Meadway Closes also, but the intention remained stillborn.)

Ascend the steps into Heathgate, and look back at the Extension.

Except for the Changing Rooms (and in fact a barn had once stood at that spot), the view is virtually unchanged since it was farmland in the nineteenth century, and is worth savouring for a moment.

The intended view from Linnell Close, designed by Guy Dawber, a founder of the Council for the Protection of Rural England. The mansion on the left was never built, and so the vista was never achieved.

Retrace your way down the steps, turning right to resume your way alongside the Great Wall.

Each of the gazebos is different, but are all exemplars of the Arts and Crafts Movement.

When you reach the penultimate gazebo before reaching Hampstead Way, turn left and cross Bush Field to rejoin the path you were on before turning off to visit the Great Wall, as it emerges from behind the hedgerow.

You will note that the stream (and hedgerow) in fact doglegs under the path. The hedgerow is very old, probably at least medieval. There are more than fifteen different species in this hedgerow, a strong indicator of its antiquity, including oak, ash, hawthorn, blackthorn (in Cobbett's words, 'excellent for the making of hedges'), field maple and wilding apple. Although the present trees are not particularly old, the presence of woodland hawthorn (distinguished most easily from the ordinary hawthorn by its more

On reaching the changing rooms, turn right up the main track, into Cart Path Field.

This, of course, is the continuation of the track from Wild Hatch, lined on its right side by fine pedunculate oaks and another wild service tree.

These probably marked the very edge of Wyldes Wood felled by John Slannyng.

Continue up through Pond Field.

On your right lies what is now called Children's Enclosure Field, but was part of Lower Weild Pightle. Until the Second World War sheep were grazed on the Extension, and folded into the Children's Enclosure Field at night.

Continue into Southern Rough.

Immediately to your left stands a fountain in memory of Walter Field. Field (1837-1901) was a painter and an Associate of the Royal Society of Painters in Watercolours (hence ARWS). Field was a lifelong Hampstead man. His father lived at Squire's Mount, while he lived where The Pryors flats now stand on East Heath Rd. But Field had no connection with Wyldes. Why is his memorial here? Field's sister, Emily, had been a founder of the Hampstead Heath Protection Society and joint-founder with Henrietta Barnett of the Heath Extension Council. It seems she had the memorial fountain quickly erected in early 1907 before the LCC could gainsay her.

On your right is 'Upper Weild Pightle'. 'Pightle' – an impressively arcane agricultural term – means a small enclosure or parcel, often of arable land. It suggests that while we have no record of these fields being anything but pasture or meadow, at some stage the two 'pightles' may have been under the plough.

Continue walking up the track, which bears to the right.

On your left just before the horse track stands a group of trees dominated by elm suckers. It marks Wildwood, or Tooley's Farm, a group of rather ramshackle buildings still standing in 1907, but which were dismantled by the LCC. Three generations of Tooleys worked 75 acres of the Wyldes estate from here for much of the nineteenth century.

Continue along the track, crossing Wildwood Road, and up the track, to turn right.

As you turn right along in front of the houses, note the bank with the oak tree on the corner by the house which marks the Saxon boundary between Hendon and Hampstead. The boundary runs through the gardens along the front edge of the row of houses.

The entrance to Tooley's Farm, 1887, twenty years before Wildwood Road was laid past the gate.

Stop at the third and fourth houses, Wyldes and Old Wyldes.

These are the farm house and buildings for the Wyldes estate. Old Wyldes was probably built in the early seventeenth century. There is no evidence of a building preceding it, and it is possible that since so much was still woodland before the mid-sixteenth century, that there had been no need of farm buildings. Siting the farmhouse for the estate here suggests several things: that it was built before the acquisition of the larger Temple Fortune estate to the north; that the easiest access to the estate was from North End.

The part which is now called Wyldes was a barn constructed in the eighteenth century and subsequently converted for domestic use. As can be seen from the plaque, Old Wyldes was home to John Linnell, the painter, from 1823-1827. Linnell's great friend William Blake often visited him here, and acquired a great affection for the Heath. While working on Dante's *Divine Comedy* he christened some nearby trees 'the Dante Wood', probably Turner's Firs towards the Spaniards (see p.37).

Wyldes became home to Raymond Unwin when he was chosen to design the layout for Hampstead Garden Suburb. Although the Suburb became inhabited largely by a professional class, Unwin had been drawn to the original project because of its social dimension. His ambition had always been to design a decent and uplifting environment in which 'working class' people could live. Indeed, quite by chance he had met Samuel Barnett twenty years earlier in Oxford. Barnett had dissuaded him from the priesthood since he was concerned more by human suffering than by sin. Neither suspected their paths would cross again.

Hampstead Garden Suburb never really fulfilled its purpose as a neighbourhood 'for all classes'. A severe shortage of money was the major factor. There was always pressure to maximise income, and that meant selling to richer people in order to keep the project going. Besides, the few 'artisan's dwellings' that were built were so beautifully architected that they quickly attracted young professional people. Thus the guidelines intended to guarantee a wide social mix rapidly foundered, and the suburb became what it is today, a professional middle class neighbourhood.

Bibliography

PUBLISHED

Adams, Gene, 'Dido Elizabeth Belle: a black girl at Kenwood', *Camden History Review*, No. 12, 1984.

Baines, F.E., *Records of the Manor, Parish and Borough of Hampstead*, 1890.

Barratt, Thomas J, *The Annals of Hampstead*, 1912.

Barton, Nicholas, *The Lost Rivers of London*, 1962.

Carswell, John, *The Saving of Kenwood and the Northern Heights*, 1992.

Collins, D., and Lorimer, D. (editors) *Excavations at the Mesolithic Site on West heath, 1976-1981*, Hendon and District Archaeological Society.

Farmer, Alan, *Hampstead Heath*, 1984.

Gerard, John, *The Herball, or General Historie of Plantes*, 1597.

Gilmour, J.S.L., *Thomas Johnson: Botanical Journeys in Kent and Hampstead*, 1629-32, 1972.

Hampstead Scientific Society, *Hampstead Heath: Its Geology and Natural History*, 1913.

Hoskins, W.G., *The Making of the English Landscape*, 1955.

Howitt, William, *The Northern Heights of London*, 1869.

Ikin, C.W., *Hampstead Heath: How the Heath was saved for the Public*, 1985.

Ikin, C.W. *Hampstead Garden Suburb: Dreams and Realities*, 1990.

Kennedy, J., *The Manor and Parish Church of Hampstead*, 1906.

Lovell, P.W., and Marcham, W. McB., *The Village of Highgate (The Parish of St Pancras Pt. I)* (Survey of London, vol. xvii), 1936.

Lloyd, J.H., *Caen Wood and its Associations*, 1892.

Mabey, Richard, *Flora Britannica*, 1996.

Miller, Mervyn, and Gray, A Stuart, *Hampstead Garden Suburb*, 1992.

Mitchell, Alan, *A Field Guide to the Trees of Britain and Northern Europe*, 1974.

Park, John James, *The Topography and Natural History of Hampstead*, 1814.

Potter, George W., *Hampstead Wells*, 1904.

Rackham, Oliver, *The History of the Countryside*, 1986.

Rackham, Oliver, *Trees and Woodlands in the British Landscape*, 1976, revised 1990.

Richardson, John, *Highgate: Its History since the Fifteenth Century*, 1983.

Rosenthal, Michael, *Constable: The Painter and his Landscape*, 1983.

Simon, Jacob, 'Humphry Repton at Kenwood: A Missing Red Book', *Camden History Review*, no. 11, 1984.

Stokes, Malcolm, *Highgate Hunting Ground*, 1984.

Stokes, Malcolm, *A Walk along Ancient Boundaries in Kenwood*, 1995.

Stow, John, *A Survey of London Written in the Year 1598*, 1876.

Sullivan, David, *The Westminster Corridor: The Anglo-Saxon story of Westminster Abbey and its lands in Middlesex*, 1994.

Sullivan, David, 'Hamlet on the upgrade', *Hampstead and Highgate Express*, 25 May 1979.

Thompson, F.M.L., *Hampstead: Building a Borough, 1650-1964*, 1974.

Tindall, Gillian, *The Fields Beneath*, 1985.

Town Planning and Modern Architecture at the Hampstead Garden Suburb, 1909.

Venning, Philip, *Wyldes: A New History*, cyclostyled, 1977.

Victoria County History, *Middlesex*.

UNPUBLISHED

Ikin, C.W., 'Three younger sons between Hampstead and Highgate' unpublished, nd.

Land Use Consultants, 'Hampstead Heath' (various surveys), 1992-1995.

Vaughan, Anthony, 'Survey of the Heath Extension, 1996-97' for the London Natural History Society (unpublished, nd).

Wright, Jeremy, 'Hampstead Heath Extension: concordance of field numbers', cyclostyled, nd.

Index